ARBOREAL THOUGHT

A Neophyte's Spirit - Willingly Hopeful with a Forward-Looking Disposition

PHILIP D. REISNER

ARBOREAL THOUGHT

Weightless Spirits Willingly Fly with a Persuasive,
Heavenly Embrace

PHILLIP D. REISNER

Also by Phillip D. Reisner

Whispering

Time Remnants

Letters To Angela

I See Movies in My Head

Dichotomy

Two Days in Superior Court One

Order this book online at www.trafford.com
or email orders@trafford.com

Most Trafford titles are also available at major online book retailers.

Print information available on the last page.

ISBN: 978-1-4907-8514-1 (sc)
ISBN: 978-1-4907-8515-8 (hc)
ISBN: 978-1-4907-8521-9 (e)

Library of Congress Control Number: 2017915428

Trafford rev. 10/06/2017

www.trafford.com

North America & international
toll-free: 1 888 232 4444 (USA & Canada)
fax: 812 355 4082

Preface

My idea of "Arboreal Thought" is an analogy based on the "Arboreal Hypothesis" that suggests a ground-running biped of some kind adapted itself to living in trees. The hypothesis suggests that the biped began climbing trees, then leaping branches, then parachuting branches and finally developing feathered flapping wings to fly.

Wikipedia, http://en.wikipedia.org/wiki/Origin of birds, defines the hypothesis as the following:

"Also known as the "from the trees down" hypothesis. Most versions of the arboreal hypothesis state that the ancestors of birds were very small dinosaurs that lived in trees, springing from branch to branch. This small dinosaur already had feathers, which were co-opted by evolution to produce longer, stiffer forms that were useful in aerodynamics, eventually producing wings. Wings would have then evolved and become increasingly refined as devices to give the leaper more control, to parachute, to glide, and to fly in stepwise fashion."

I suggest by comparison that a human mind first ground runs as a newborn; then develops a mind over time that can fly like an eagle, soar with ease and grace, and has no limits for future imagining and deep thinking. Arboreal thought is free, limitless and uninhibited. It is aerodynamic thought like an eagle's body grounded by a human's dynamic mind. A hypothesis is only an idea based on some logic or philosophy that has merit. My writing about life experiences tests my arboreal thought idea. My aggregated thoughts are generally only ideas that are untested and unproven. They are just one man's thoughts accrued over many years. I'm simply trying to advance thought as uninhibited conjecture. I believe most people can advance their thought process and promote it with others' help; through encountered experience they develop an ability to mentally soar like an eagle. We rise and fall from birth to death, and at some point, in our lives are capable of soaring. We reach a mental zenith where miracles are possible and dreams get satisfied. Admittedly, some people dream larger and higher than others. Many of us in our own little way seem to flirt with genius a few times in our lives. A few of us do more than flirt, but enable greatness, bear fruit and thus share unearned blessings.

How many of us will remain biped crawling and how many will mentally soar like an eagle? I sometimes pretend to mentally soar like an eagle with no limitations or inhibitions. I, however, fear my zenith has come and gone, and yet I am able to share some wisdom gained from execution of own arboreal thought. I like to think I have developed a theory and philosophy of life that is useful for others. My "Arboreal Thought" hopefully surfaces through my writing. Welcome to my pretentious world.

Most everyone has insignificantly and personally created myths and traditions that are part of their very essence. Some people are truly larger than life, yet wish only simple love from surrounding others. A few lucky people are somewhat legendary to friends and family, modestly held within a small social circle. They are usually greater and more important than they believe themselves to be. The few stories that get passed down to the next generation as personal history are likely to be true and are usually based on admired skills, talents or feats.

Long established actions or behavior patterns are often handed down, and thus establish beliefs and values for speculation. Most everyone practices minimum personal mythology one way or another. I prefer to concentrate on positive myths and traditions within the confines of this book. I, like most people, have no great myths to share, only humble, personal, insignificant folklore; after all I am not important enough to contribute greatness, but can flirt with speculation and arboreal thought.

If you were to write a book about yourself, what would you include? You could look at your last resume and find ideas for personal myths or maybe look at a photo album for thought provoking memories. All you need are some people, places or things to jog your memory. You could also ask family and friends for their opinion of you. That might be interesting. Your personal myths and traditions will surely surface. I suspect you will see yourself and your life with a different perspective. I believe you will perceive yourself as being more important than you thought.

We are determined important by the relationships we have cultivated and how we have affected other people; of course, we should look for positive influences. If positive impacts prove to be not present, then it is never too late to establish positive myths and traditions. We are unimportant in the grand scheme of things, but are personally important to ourselves and can become important through time and influence on others. We gain true importance from other people's opinions of ourselves. You should listen to others and yourself; write your own book and assess your life through personal myths and traditions.

I want to share some personal significant mythology with you, and through sharing, help you construct your own poetic folklore book. We shall together find our importance in retrospect. History is the best evaluator of everything. Our short-term history is valuable while living and after death.

It is possible to provoke the universe into existence even after passing from Earth as others left behind indirectly remember us through mutual history and artifacts. We will leave Earth for certain, becoming again part of the universal essence of "Things." Remember well, for all is in your soul suitcase waiting for heavenly confirmation; but that is another story.

If you have read other books of mine, you learned that I believe our soul is like a suitcase, where we collect the history of everything physically and intellectually learned, experienced and felt. We must save our earthly baggage collection. God will collect our spirit, but it is our responsibility to save our soul and show its contents to Him when returning to heaven. I'm sure we will make him smile and frown. We should pray for more smiles than frowns while showing our collected self-mythology.

So, write your book for earthly and heavenly inspection, for family and Godly inspection. Who knows, maybe the memory of you will live more than a few passing generations. Good luck on that thing.

Life matters little if lived without self-expression and liberty. Life is cheap if constructed from pretentious thought, knowledge and philosophy. A thoughtful deed given with realized awareness is less valuable than one accomplished with triumphant ignorance, and yet private self-awareness is required for true unaware public giving. Humility is balancing actions on a sharp awareness fulcrum. One's life evaluation is the responsibility of others.

Academia is a wonderful foundation for life, but has no walls or roof. Self-construction is only possible through experience and wisdom. Each person must write own story in own way about own specialties.

Life, liberty and the pursuit of happiness is a spiritual thing on Earth, but surely based on heavenly advice. A collection of personal life poems, written or unwritten, gives legitimacy and proof of one's life. Some types of ignorance can be beneficial if practiced with the right state of mind. Life is better lived by following most rules, but practiced with a mythical and liberated mind.

Contents

Practicing Self Mythology

Chapter I - Embracing Mind

Chapter II - Inventing Grace

Chapter III - Measuring Moments

Chapter IV - Feeling Marvelous

Chapter V - Accepting Motion

The Art of Self Liberation

Chapter VI - Saving Memories

Chapter VII - Hearing Music

Chapter VIII - Finding Maturity

Chapter IX - Using Mentality

Chapter X - Cherishing Moods

Part 1

Practicing Self Mythology

Introduction

Lingering gray thoughts tease a mind to prevail, to enlighten and make known time's fleeting mythology.

Bright, heated passion recklessly burns and rejoices. It seeks fulfillment at any cost while hindering cool remembrance. Most humans beg for more life and plead for silent traditions to remain and will not easily succumb to death's engulfing hunger.

Compassionate mythology too often pauses in middle barren ground and cannot satisfy loving acceptance of gaining importance. However, in transitory grace, we all conquer and attend to God's eclipsing truth.

We all contribute to His mystical music and graceful poetry one way or another. Maybe we contribute with a single note or a whole song. Maybe we contribute with a few words or a complete book of hopeful wisdom. Somehow, some way, we are finally laid to rest with a song of our own making. Personal myth and reality depends on how we compose life.

Chapter I

Embracing Mind

I Remember

I recall a yellow room with
white curtains frolicking
in morning sunlight with
two-month old awareness.
I recall being awake and
waiting mother's assuring arms.
I recall colic crying, naively
yearning for attention and
face against a soft breast.
It's tricky to remember life
at a fledgling age, but
once sensed and recorded,
it is wondrously recalled.
Linked mind pictures and
movies are like a thousand
yellow rooms, white curtains
and a free mind reflecting.

2

I recall a small white house
on a hill above a quiet street.
A concrete wall foils erosion.
Modest white house waits
playing in tall green grass
in a gentle summer breeze.
An old brick grocery store a
few blocks away, with a
tattered screen door,
invites my entrance.
A colorful painted parrot
advertises bread on a
screened door that catches
my eye before entering

when two years old.
I didn't understand then,
but recognized and
put meaning to it later.

3

I recall a country house,
room at top of long stairs,
bed nestled beneath a
slanted ceiling, against a
painted blue secure wall and
morning windowed sunlight
waking me during summer.
I recall hiding eyes and
wishing to never leave
that wonderful secure place,
even though sister tormented.
I once retaliated with an
old metal pulley, striking
her head at five years old.
I yet see blood and hear
shameful words in mind.
I caused pain and suffering
and never said, "sorry."

4

I surely recall riding a
yellow school bus,
often being asked to
sit on a hot heater
next to Miss Myrtle
for misbehaving.
I remember scrambling
from seat to seat to avoid
awesome Nadine Oliver,
who pursued innocent me,
threatening to kiss me.

I was a ten-year-old kid,
she was a beautiful
seventeen-year-old woman.
I stupidly avoided her
full lips and flowing red hair.
I recall heat and dusty
gravel roads while passing
farm houses and barns,
daily stopping for friends
Dennis, Don, "Peely" Paul.
I was glad to not ride that
school bus when sixteen,
smugly driving own car.

5

I clearly remember
leaning against my black
fifty-four, two door Ford
with a James Dean attitude,
just after movie experiencing
Rebel Without a Cause at
impressionable age sixteen.
Warm sun and gentle breezes
altered my long hair and
turned-up collar disposition.
I whispered love words to
Jackie Thompson before and
after school while remaining
cool and delight contained
when in her charming presence.
Red unchanged school
building bricks looked new,
inside stare steps looked old.
A round, metal fire escape

extended two stories up and
provided a means to crawl
upward and into a hallway.
I played basketball during
eleven-thirty activity period,
then ate a huge amount of
cafeteria peanut butter and
jelly sandwiches at lunch.

6

I recall my favorite teacher
Mr. Turner who taught
me more than biology, and
judging farm animals and
grain with skillful success.
I once ate two dozen extra
night class yeast donuts with
classmates before his
first period biology class,
getting sick and burping
donuts for awkward hours.
Mr. Turner constantly ate
Tums to quell stomach acid;
we surely helped create it by
just being high school kids.
I yearly bought winning Black
Angus 4-H steers from him.

7

I recall at my graduation
Albert Laforge, our janitor,
saying he was surprised
I made it and me saying,
"It's no big thing."
I went on to earn BS and

MS degrees, and thought
they also were no big thing.
It was as if life flowed
through open windows and
I ignorantly thought
living was effortless and
in my mind, no big thing.
I was later proud of
those accomplishments,
vividly brain recorded and
amazingly mind recalled.

8

I never lost ability to
record and recall
experiences that often
became wisdom through
pictures and movies
in my mystical head.
I delight in memories
of people, places and
things historically stored
in heart, mind and soul.
Melancholy sometimes
seizes my whole being,
reminding of success,
failure and love.

Faint Whispers

In a bedroom at
three o-clock am,
I warily walked
in near darkness
with moonlight
passing through
dirty windows.

A deep
glass bowl of
collected shells
levitated and
got placed
on a nearby
dresser top.
I was surely
not alone with
spirits near
as close as
nose's end.

I scolded
my hands for
not clasping.
My carelessly
painted mind
showed weakness.
Reluctant ears
fought sound
of vibrating
ghosts circling.
Weight of
butterfly wings
on shoulders

pressed kindly.
I heard angels
cast lots for
my soul.
My neck hair
straightened,
fear forced
internal search
of own spirit
hanging in
latent limbo.

On bended knee
I clasped hands,
bent stiff neck
towards floor and
prayed for
soul protection.
I heard
faint whispers
of "hallelujah,
hallelujah" as
morning came
suddenly soon.

Sunlight
replaced
moon light.
Hope replaced
anxiety.
I replaced
sea shell
bowl with
new thought.

Dirt

It's strange
how thoughts
many times
linger as if
they belong
in mind, as if
they grow to
like it there,
wishing not
another
place to be.

Good
thoughts are
like teasing
plants,
sprouting
in thought,
maturing in
mind dirt,
influencing a
blossoming
life philosophy.

Bad
thoughts are
like weeds
that need
hoeing and
pulling, and if
tended to

will in mind
dissipate as
forgotten
organic matter.

Learned
thoughts are
like flowers
that bloom,
cause joy and
in time get
remembered as
knowledge
gained along
time's never
forgotten way.

Sentimental
thoughts
linger as if
suitable
in heart,
conveye d and
shared as
joy with an
emotional,
collecting
soul.

*Thoughts briefly pass precious time, occupy minor space
and like human beings, silently die trying to stay alive.*

Dismal Thoughts

Gloomy ideas
flood body
and mind as
heart aches and
soul gasps.

Tender history
emerges as
vulnerability
unravels
found solace.

Heaven opens to
adored those
allowing passion
to occur from
covert suffering.

Love spans a
billion miles
through a
thin time and
space shield.

Spirits heal
broken souls
like a potter's
shattered vase
gets repaired.

Art Work

Art pieces placed
about my home are
like precious jewels
gracefully decorating
my existence.
They perhaps mean
little to others
who stroll past
walls or glance at
cabinet shelves.

What is art?

On walls and
glass shelves,
reside collected
artful objects
speaking for me,
telling who I am.
They mark
Earth time,
give value to
artfully gathered
soul pieces during
trials and errors.

What is sensed value?

Value makes
no mark on an
insignificant,
uninvested world.
I'm not rich with
savings or reserves,

but am abound
with invested well
timed symbols
that historically
define, refine and
remind my soul.

What is time well spent?

So, appreciate
my symbolic home
in heart and eye.
See my
wondering way
towards heaven's
gate through
collected art
that hangs and
sits silently, yet
for me personally
speaks loudly.

Do we mark our path to heaven?

Ash and Stone

I silently
linger in a
melancholy place,
recalling
passing flowers and
how they never
truly leave, but
transform all
they touch, and
then become
ash memories.

A better gardener
I wish to be,
gentle and forgiving
with natural ways,
practicing God's
given instructions,
giving love and
planting with more
spiritual awareness.

I wish to be
more mindful,
pray ahead in
morning's
rousing light and
endlessly say
"I love you"
in night's
tough darkness.

I wish to pay
attention to

detail while
cultivating
family grain and
allowing golden
soulful wheat to
wave well until
harvest time.

I lightly lay
living flowers
on a casket,
September twenty-six,
nineteen-ninety-six,
while forever
sleeping wheat
waits another
cyclical planting.

Gardeners and
farmers stand
soundlessly,
ruefully praying
too late for
sun and rain at
mid-day zenith.

I wish to be
more mindful,
pray ahead in
morning's
rousing light and
endlessly say
"I love you"
in night's
tough darkness.

Cobalt Eyes

In widen
mind corner
at a crossroads,
a cobalt eyed,
black clad
evil entity
sought
my attention.
Soul selling
came to mind.

Bartering and
trading own
value was
frightening.
My mind
got pelted
with hellish
crystal hail
while in a
vicious storm.

Multi colored
thoughts
artfully sketched
my mind like
playing card
faces of a stacked
psyche deck.
A spade of
aces advocated
hopelessness.

A dark
evil being with
cobalt eyes
captivated a
shrinking fool.
My courage and
temperament
fought weakly.
I believed in
no escape.

o

Dream remnants
reluctantly linger,
faint images float
like morning fog
caressing mind.
Reality declares a
new direction
as a thousand
satanic thoughts
percolate softly,
manipulating and
tainting intellect.

Caldron surface
reflects shadowy
lighted room
from clear black
mirrored water.
Cobalt eyes
slowly disappear.
I am alone and
wisely whisper,
"let it be, let it be."

Come Quickly

Time sets day upon day as
life evolves under a
celestial carpenter's eye.
His holy tools fasten
survival bulwark together.
Wood, steel and stone,
mind, soul and spirit coalesce.

Through every door
comes friend and foe,
sweet fruit and bitter root.
Time and spirituality will
reveal mansion or shack,
placed and built in a minute
or a hundred lived years.

o

Come, pass through
my home with pleasure,
seeking not my art or
treasured gain, but find
comfort sitting on a
shaded porch swing in an
inviting friendly space.

o

He came with
hunger for
my soul like a
violent storm,
wishing to eat

passive daylight.
His cobalt eyes
watched in black
evil expression,
seeking my awareness

In tempest chaos a
battle ensued for
my transient
mind, soul and
everlasting spirit.
I clearly witnessed
own calm essence
sternly converse
with evil through a
heavenly window.

Dry Wind

Propelling dry
morning air
carries sound of
bells tolling and
silent evaporating
dew drops on
green grass resting.
It exposes flaws as
certain, acceptable
worldly changes.

If dew drops
possessed a
harmonic say,
church organs
would play
hallelujah music at
dawn and make
saints dance.

If wind and
dew drops
together
were family,
wind would send
precious dew to
dry high planes
praying for
blessed rain.

Nature's breath embraces life with variable
vibrations that sustain God's initial voice.

If they
were preachers,
wind and dew
would surely
know for what
humans pray and
what music brings
happiness.

If both had
mouths and
could speak,
they would
flaunt beauty and
grace as might
poets and
song writers.

If they
could tell time,
they would act
like polite clocks
grasping
cruel time to
measure wind
speed and distance.

If they
were brothers,
they would not
seek revenge and
would settle
disputes with
tough patience.

If they
were birds,
they would
dry leaves and
fan grass with
collective wings
serving as
nature's breath.

If they
were mothers,
they would
embrace life with
vibrations of
internal bells to
propagate
future generations.

And if wind and
dew drops
were Angels,
they would
acknowledge
counseling from
tireless sun and
spiritually share
existence at dawn.

Nature's breath embraces life with variable
vibrations that sustain God's initial voice.

Glorious

I ignite a
small brush pile
near river's bank
consisting of
dead limbs,
scrap wood and
fallen leaves.
Smoke rolls
across lazy water
allowing
true freedom
unification of
two banks,
water flow and
directing wind's
soft touch.
Freedom, wood,
fire and I are
God's servants
in this melding.

As I observe
spiritual smoke
billowing and
mysteriously moving
down river,
I cannot help,
but build a
similar fire in mind,
artfully coalescing
thought and
treasured memories.
My personal history is
set ablaze with

splendid liberty,
gloriously enjoining
freedom's rise.
My spirit and
soul rejoice,
remaining so
until fire and
river calm as
whole time
becomes a moment,
my ever moment.

God Must Surely Love

I think about cartoon characters I've known and
    people bent on uniqueness without intention.

I think about memorable faces and bodies, about
    speech patterns and accents echoing in mind.

I think about brilliance and stupidity, grace and
    awkwardness filling my responsive head.

I think about noses, short legs, big bellies and
    attributes that cause ordinary folks to be rare.

I think about story telling ways and methods, and
    listening with ease of ear and excitement.

I think about grace and demeanor that causes
    me to believe I could also gracefully dance.

Oh and yes, those smiles and frowns tell much,
    they often cause me to behave and misbehave.

I have comic books, movies and TV shows in
    my head that instigate ideas, stories and events.

I think about human nature traits that cause me to
    slightly love humanity like God must greatly love.

I Fold My Hands

I sit in stillness gazing
with open hands and
eyes in dusky light.
My working hands
clutch to build and
fold mind to pray.
I see history and
read graceful lines
earned by work.
My whole cosmos
reveals itself by a
moment's glance
at precious hands.
I humbly sense
self-worth by
stroking face and
feeling whiskered
varied roughness.
I again fold
my prayerful
reverence giving,
working hands.
I lack much, yet
appreciation own
honest worth.
And, by a faint
innermost light,
I see farther than
thought possible.
My mind contains
poetic insight
created through
practice and toil.

A Life Element

Living without
sadness is a
luxury only
those who die
young escape.

But you see,
sadness is a
soft gauze that
protects with
real reasoning.

It causes hurts
to mend and
allows our
likenesses to
jointly bound.

It makes us
repose and
sleep, and
comfortably
be alone.

Melancholy is
sadness born,
its comparison
keeps alive past
graceful times.

It makes
us remember
events and
life pieces that
mend souls.

We don't
fall apart,
or get broken
from melancholy
thought.

We're humbled
through sadness
contrasting
elements to never
be forgotten.

Melancholy care
fabricates a
colorful soul
speckled with
sadness elements.

I Saw

I saw my soul's
disposition as a
flat blue lake
while yesterday
reflecting.
Hands clasped,
wisdom seeped,
mind shared
while recalling
life experiences.
Remembrance
brushed and
willingly combed
evoked efforts.
Time sought
what could be
defined while
wisdom escaped
understanding.
I threatened
to dive into clear
blue water and
disturb true image,
but that meant
entering soul and
that scared me so.

o

I tend my garden in
late afternoon sun,
sighing good-bye to
tree shadows,
creeping across

tilled dark soil.
They seem, like
giant veined hands,
wishing to scoop
innocent dirt.
Rich pungent
aroma seeps,
filling air,
reminding of
past gardens.

o

Family garden
memories capture
imagination, like
mother's hands,
plunging deep into
rich organic essence.

Thoughts of her
sun tanned arms and
big garden hat,
remind as if
she never left
producing Earth.

I see her bending,
weeding, hoeing and
garden assessing.
My mind floods,
making heart plead
for revived days.

I see her within
midst of green
vegetation,

selecting 4-H
best of show for a
county fair exhibit.

I feel hands hoeing,
sweat beading and
back aching.
I find joy in
thinking about
growing a garden.

I yet till soil with
my mother
in loving mind
even though,
she has long
passed to heaven.

Familiar aches and
discomforts are
good reminders of
labor served and
mother loved on
our green Earth.

Last Candle

I burned
last candle,
used last match,
slept beside lover
one last time
while music
played and
fanned air rushed
over nakedness
one last time.

I laid at night
like a silent
Easter Island statue,
half buried in thought,
waiting for
someone to return.
I felt spiritual beings
gather my arms and
gently pull me
upward as if
out of heavy sand.

I gained legs
to walk, to run,
to explore
my mental island.
I groped in
unforgiving darkness.
It was strange
how a moon-less night
sought no light and a
mind-less world
desired no relief.

I fumbled in
despair and
found a candle,
then a match.
My darkened world
became lighted
again with an
instant flash of
holiness.
I heard a
knock at
my front door,
opened it and
stood with
outstretched arms.
I saw
my Easter Island
counterpart,
holding an ancient
glowing tablet.

She took hand,
kissed lips and
held me
one more time.
I groped
no longer for
match or
candle, and
in my soul
rose a
light and a
love that would
last forever.

Last Mile Walked

A bell called
my name,
then spoke
common words.
Silent frost
gathered on
my shoulders.
I shuttered.
Time decorated
my presence in
formal regard.
A speaker
pulled at
my shirttail mind,
pulling towards a
mystical reward.
It resonated
during sleepless night.

Deep purple
shaded
my eyes as
sleep evaded.
It fashioned
myself as a saint
walking a last path.
I heard bell toll,
softly speak,
reminding me of
its presence.
It exposed
last mile to walk.
I removed
my frosty shirt,

exposing skin,
soon becoming
unusually warm.

I walked with
great self-awareness.
I climbed a mountain,
swam an ocean and
finally, lay resting.
I heard all with
understanding,
shed all clothing,
stood naked with
no embarrassment.
Someone placed a
purple shroud
on my shoulders.
Bell signaled
midnight,
time to sleep,
felt last vibration.
I then slept well
in amiable repose.
I embraced
vigilant angels
who said, "well done."

Membrane Away

I stretch arms in
Open invitation.
I expose heart to
Spiritual will.
My soul cries for help.
I want to be
Ghost connected.

Ghosts do come and
Stand beside me.
I fold prayerful hands.
Spiritual world is a
Membrane away.
Upon my essence
It presses.

Ghosts surround.
I'm linked to
Cosmic knowledge,
Yet cannot grasp as
Frustration seeps.
Most is beyond mind.
I need more faith.

I rush towards
Mountain climbed,
Ocean swam,
Membrane crossed and
Got ghost guided
Towards cosmic
Other side of midnight.

Moist Air

Moist poetic
apprentice air
disturbs
my searching
collective soul;
like a rain filled
teaching cloud,
I seek a place to
shed tears on a
parched essence.
I franticly search
for more than a
transcendental
expression place of
earthly time and
desperate space.

I'll probably be known as a momentary event,
like a consumed match to be hastily discarded.

.

I fear being a
fading light
upon pages of
foolishly written
poetry books.
No matter analogy,
I shall inevitably
be only a
down payment of a
brief flicker,
too soon consumed
like moist air on
dusty earth.
I assuredly

pray to be an
innocent spirit
drifting towards
believed infinity,
flowing towards
that holy place
where spirit and
soul explains
earthly experience
to God.

I'll probably be known as a momentary event,
like a consumed match to be hastily discarded.

Mean Rain Drops

Cold mean rain drops
beat on my head to
waken dull attention.
It's like ever dripping
water hitting a pail that
eventually reshapes
rigid righteousness.
Thoughts with no
agenda bend thirsty,
pursuing mind.

In evolving world
where right and wrong
distorts reality equally,
time erodes sure as a
security wall crumbles.
I run towards clear sky,
afraid that rain clouds
might alter my shape.
I can't guess nature or
predict its intention.

I finally approach
accumulated rain drops,
count ocean waves as
time passes through me.
I collect aware seconds,
place them in pocket and
drink rain from a pail.
I, however, collect time
in a loosely woven basket,
near ocean's salty mirth.

Mindful America

America, America are you
so different than a well-planned,
created fireplace that warms
hearts, minds and souls with diverse
stones to make one great nation?

o

Labor melded cosmic art and
earthly purpose into a heap of
creek stones mortared together
to heat a cabin and strengthen life,
liberty and pursuit of happiness.

All felt secure in that little cabin,
smiling from joy while gazing at
diverse creek rock application
crafted into an artful air drawing
fireplace serving many demands.

o

America, America are you
so different than a well-planned,
created fireplace that warms
hearts, minds and soul with diverse
stones to make one great nation?

Chapter II

Inventing Grace

Earned Space

I can't be
wholly amiss,
so listen to
my song.
Grace whispers
in my head and
shakes free a
courageous
haunting melody.

Only God
knows where
I can hide
in this place of
touching charm.
I cannot
embrace life,
when it won't
stand still.

Take my hand,
lead me into
lighted way, for
it's mighty dark.
I'll not sleep
until ending
song meets
discovered
arising melody.

My Hands

I brought
hands before
wanton eyes, and
spoke to them as if
they were friends,
could save my life,
were possibly holy.
I then reached for
heaven with those
abused hands,
holy trusted them.
Into heart
poured spirits and
angelic emissaries,
sharing righteous
wisdom.

I bent to
humble knees and
thanked hands for
their intention with
no apprehension.
They gathered
knowledge like a
hundred flowers,
placed bouquet in
childlike mind while
spirits evoked
understanding.
I coordinated
labored hands with
eyes and mind, and
became saintly.

My Own Gray Stone

A gray stone
fills my eyes,
looking at
where silence
hides grief.
History enters
blue eyes and
muddles mind.

I gaze
eastwardly,
face morning sun,
whisper angry,
graphic words.
That decisively
placed stone
seems to listen.

Spirits wash
over and
around me,
touch cheek,
brush lips;
warm breeze
invades and
cleanses mind.

Gray stone
embraces placed
wilted flowers

helplessly laying
in time's
strewn affair
because time
waits for no one.

Rain kisses and
sun caresses,
dead flowers fall
to waiting Earth;
precious organic
substance invites
submerged peace
in a passion grave.

Life's wilted
flowers become
another season as
one gray stone
communicates,
teaches day and
night answers of
sunlight and rain.

One gray stone
exists long after
flowers, flesh and
seasons are gone;
only mind yet
illustrates a cosmos
rejoicing beyond
spiritual ascension.

My Quilt

My quilting mind,
stitches and
sews carefully,
ages and frays
unwittingly well.
New segments
organize while
timeworn ones
disappear daily.
My momentarily
completed quilt
fears getting folded
and put away in
some dark drawer.

I as a human
pray to slip away
some day to a
holy place like a
striking quilt
finally completed.
I shall reminisce
dear time and
materials sown
into a unique
living mosaic.
I shall display
my quilted soul
for God's approval.

Night Grapes

Night hides
like a painter's
artless pallet
awaiting natural
artist humility.
It dissolves
colors with a
black silent
shadowy stroke.
Night has no
hidden need or
fragile love for
light's growth.

Night grows
grapes as
benevolent gifts
in light's absence.
Night allows
flowing juice of
future wine to
muse existence
while day brings
squeezing and
fermenting
violence.
Humble night
grapes wait
bright tomorrow's
fateful light.

Life hides in
night's cloaking
respite as

grapes wait in
colorless repose.
It hides grape
attributes and
potential allure.
Day radiates
glorious colors with
night's pleading
contrast reward.
Day defines
passion and paints
worthiness with
night's caress.

o

Like a thorny
rose creeper
seeks own nightly
reclamation, a
small night grape
waits tomorrow's
final illumination.

Each personally
painted portrait
always requires
light and darkness.
Every living
creature is a
painter's pallet
exhibiting artistic
excellence.

Night's Full Moon

*I'm a graceful essence from far beyond cosmic planets and
stars coming at light speed searching for a place to belong.*

I'm a bit of
heavenly hoard
sent to earth.
I'm a speck
of paradise
mortally placed
as a spiritual
human being.
I came from
beyond faithful
cosmic moons,
planets and
stars that now
stare back from
where I came.

As night's
full moonlight
strikes eyes and
stars gaze back,
wondrous thoughts
come to mind as
divine whispered
poetry and prose.
Cosmic history
seeps my heart,
mind and soul
like welcomed
rain water into
thirsty soil on a
September night.

Old Guitar

An old guitar
plays no more,
sits in a corner
abandoned with
stressed and
out of tune strings.
It was once
held closely,
comforted like a
woman's breast,
softly vibrating
its soulful intrigue
through steely
life wooing,
throbbing strings.

Fashioned wood
sought expression
surely knowing
internal joy and
external sharing.
It healed
broken hearts,
mended
fractured minds,
taught peace and
patience.
It waited with
known artful
healing through
quivering ways.

On My Back Patio

I sit in my green swing,
dirty tennis shoes fixed,
worn hands lap folded,
head tranquilly resting.

I gently sway while
rhythmic metal swing
squeak hypnotizes,
mind seeks Zen state.

I invite spirits to
share opaque time
as if forever exists
in that tranquil state.

I have faith enough
to commune during a
late Friday afternoon
on my stone laid patio.

I sense a transparent
membrane dividing
aware moment from
historical amalgamation.

I willingly yield to
simple honesty and
allow penetration of a
gradually opening door.

> *Let wispy wind*
> *mystically carry me*
> *through and beyond*
> *material world.*

Let spirits lead
and teach
wisdom beyond
my earthly realm.

I traverse listening to
hypnotic swing squeak,
causing mind to plunge
into waiting possibilities.

My essence pleads in
dimmed resolve as
might my vacillating soul
discern faith and hope.

I hum timeworn words,
"Swing low sweet chariot,
com'in for to carry me home,"
to a green swing rhythm.

I find myself with
open, expanding mind,
thoughts brush soul,
reality begs mysticism.

I remain long enough
to learn and be wary of
momentary spirituality
in this engaging order.

I sit in my green swing,
dirty tennis shoes fixed,
worn hands lap folded,
head tranquilly resting.

Polite Stones

A million uncaring
stones were joined
to fabricate a
protective wall
in a world lacking
gumption mortar.

A buttress of
collective weakness
launched strength
against evil as a
million helping hands
clutched hope.

A sacred mosaic
got observed by
heavenly ghosts
for even a mountain
begins with one stone
sliding upon another.

Then countless
world restoring
humanitarians sought
peace as angels
whispered, "Halleluiah,"
above raised security.

Rainbow Hand

I caught an
imaginary rainbow
in my hand and
rotated it so as
to see all sides,
see truth of
amazing nature.
It became a
mental mirror
holding illusion.
I gazed into
willing mind,
saw another
dimensional self.
Fear faded as
confidence built.
Rainbow crystals
allowed refracted
cosmic wisdom.
My mind bent,
diffused and
stratified light.
I found self-reality,
humility and
patience with
rainbow hand.
I reasoned if
I could
catch a rainbow,
anything
was possible.

Salt on My Lips

In bright sunlight
I silently laid,
palms upward,
intensely searching
cluttered mind,
scouring soul for
spiritual answers as
foreign questions
transform mood.

Then a warm
breath kissed
suspicious face,
splashed arms and
taunted palms.
A sensed spirit
rushed realm
knowing soul.
I quested time
buried near and
far in stones, rivers,
flowers and myself.

Upon my chest
weight of butterflies
softly tickled
like a breeze
tracing hollows of
my heavy heart,
searching for
sanity and a
reason to speak.

A thin line between
here and there,
reality and fantasy,
also between
sanity and insanity,
life and death
instinctively
came to mind.

I sensed sprits
gracefully flowing
up through arms,
through chest and
into my heart.
They lingered a
few moments,
then flowed
onward
from chest,
mouth, eyes and
top of head.

Mind sought
their glitter and
magnificent lead,
for there was
no place to hide,
no place to go.
I strolled heaven
with a shimmering
spirit guiding.

"Can this last
forever?" I asked.
"Only if you die
here and now,"
spirit answered.
"You can taste
this presence for a
few moments,
then return to
your altered life."

I was left with
salty lips and
promise we would
meet again on a
mountain top with
warm breath at
my feet and a
thousand butterflies
welcoming
questioning mind.

Shiny Gray Pony

*I absorbed cosmic ways as
enduring time passed to me
some of life's covert secrets.*

I caught a
gray pony with
flying white tail and
rode westward,
leaving dreary
world behind.
I sought distant
high plains
under noon day
blazing sun.

We galloped
onward towards
far mountain peaks.
A whispering voice
from far peaks said,
"Come to a place of
sweet dreams and
fulfillment found."
Tough long days
seemed to smile.

I mystically rode
gray beauty towards
alluring distance.
I learned to speak
in poetic verse and
understand angelic
whispered prose.
I learned to sing,

create statues and
artfully arrange flowers.

I absorbed cosmic ways as
enduring time passed to me
some of life's covert secrets.

Dusk drew closer as
setting sun burned
my wide opened eyes
while watching
peaks disappear and
silhouettes grow longer.
Time resonated
obscurities that teased
imagination as reality
balanced in twilight.

Then night opened
like a giant mouth,
swallowing light with
vengeful blackness.
I gracefully fell from
my gray pony,
who disappeared
in thin night air, as
awareness sought
mind debating resolve.

I absorbed cosmic ways as
enduring time passed to me
some of life's covert secrets.

Falling, falling,
brought a new
destination with

streaking stars at
weightless feet.
Passing planets
widened intellect as
learning mind
discovered boldness
beyond known self.

Parched senses
caught and placed
my straightaway
weightless body
on white clouds
magically stirring,
melding and
supporting
thirsty brain and
hungry mind.

My gray pony
reappeared,
altered into an
angel with
shining light
enfolding her.
She showed me
my new saintly
house in cosmic
other side.

I absorbed cosmic ways as
enduring time passed to me
some of life's covert secrets.

Silent Guiding Light

An original
sparkle in
wondrous
human spirit's
eye is not from
Earth's reflection,
but from some
inner present
godly gifted
spiritual glow.

It's like a
long coastline
where beacons
beg to help anyone
approaching from
stormy seas.
And, down dark
coastal dirt roads,
other beacons
give directions.

All travelers have
an inner glow
seeking expression
of an amazing
hallelujah song,
sang in a
worthy holy place.
It's a loud stalwart
voice on a high
cliff perch singing.

Soft Velvet Blanket

I sort through lazy stars
flowing past my eyes,
naming and speaking to them
in a dead man conversing way.

When alive, I never learned a
spiritual song, felt soulful or
believed angels imparted any
benevolent divine wholeness.

I then naturally skip over
hot and cold planets,
teased cautious stars into
pausing light for a while.

No one here distinguishes
my earthly guilt or iniquities,
shortcomings or misgivings,
pains or heedful stains.

Onto an indulgent bed
I finally lay my worn self,
fall asleep on someone's lap,
allow calm peace to enter.

I'm like a newborn on a
soft majestic velvet blanket,
among planets and stars in a
divine place to linger awhile.

Sweet Days

Sweet days
happen
like a full moon
during day,
without notice.
Pleasant day
slumber can also
make dreams and
nightmares alike
come alive.

Sometimes
mind seeds
get planted,
making a heart
fear and
tears fall
into a sad garden.
Harmful weeds
smother life with
primitive hurt.

Great Gardner
lays hands on
Earth and
speaks
moon lit
flower gardens
into being.
He embellishes
sweet days with
sun and rain.

Sultry days

nurture
tilling and
planting of
dreams and
nightmares while
preserving a
restless spirit's
humble
passing of time.

In caring time
passing,
some notice
moon whether
full or not.
Day dreaming
slumber, like
silent a moon,
subtly causes a
garden to grow.

Sweet Pessimist

I cloudy sky linger as an
evil approaching alarmist.
I'm like modest bread and
wine poisoning a stomach.
Hammers and nails haunt
my blood stained cross gaze.

I bruise a perfect sky lingering,
providing begged purification.
By merely floating overhead,
I expunge grief with peace,
grow hate through love and
provide thunder with lightning.

I drench pitiful souls with
fake flowing forgiveness and
soothe spirits by giving
phony searched for answers.
Yes, I'm a pessimistic who
gives distrustful optimism.

I provide precious dove and
blue bird days infrequently
for those seeking hawk and
eagle respect on sunny days.
I'm a devilish sought creature
always cloudy sky lingering.

*Negative makes me positive
on a selected highway to hell.*

Three Horses

Cloud horses carry me
with rhythmic grace,
serene patience and
humble self-control.
I ride Trinity, passing
shadows over Earth,
never looking back.

I ride many horses,
one named Humility,
sometimes a horse
named Special, but
once in a great while
I ride a superb horse
named Spectacular.

I accrue life distance
while essence flying over
accepting still waters and
sharing green pastures.
Knowledge, wisdom and
experience is learned for
I ride spiritual horses.

Spectacular's eyes guide
blind souls seeking a
friendly cosmos wishing
to acknowledge Trinity.
Our silhouettes lead to
heaven's ultimately meld
of silent horse sense.

Thresher

Sleek gray lady
near death
who once sang a
melodic haunt, but
air in lungs
is now little.
Sailor minds
bend within
her steel like a
silenced coffin
where all still lay.
Hear her
gurgling sounds and
consoling cries.

So onward intense subduing sea,
absorb a gray nuclear submarine,
and kiss all her sailors good night.

Her heart and
back is broken.
Darkness surrounds as
spirits flow towards
someplace unexpected.
Night is falling between
here and there
in an ocean
full of creatures,
including a
gray lady with a
nuclear soul and
human spirit
long ago lost.

Understanding

My mental torch dances a playful ballet on gathering wind
that seeks grasp and empathy for daunting paths I walk.

Flickering light
reveals pathway and
harsh stumbling stones
strewn in disarray to
confound progress.

It's like my shoeless
stepping mind with
ripped toes and
slashed heals
bleeds repentance.

Influencing flames
discretely whisper
hushed sounds and
catch a mind place
on fire with advice.

To leap into
wistful flames, to
reveal soul and
cleanse myself
surely intrigues.

Night wind and
quenching rain
test my torch and
torment mind with
resisting radiance.

Soon pathway is
clear as day breaks,
absent of stones,
trepidation and
blind ignorance.

It's like a knife
slitting flesh
without pain,
seeping blood
without reason.

I am vigilant
without thought,
like a spirit
brushing cheek
without hands.

Angry clouds
cannot empty their
black rain hoard or
remind me of
inflicted wounds.

Someone paints
my mind with
innocent logic and
creates a pathway of
understanding

Vitality Flow

Sun soaks eyes
with yellow and
gold leaf colors of a
changing forest.

Yet after time and
self-discourse,
my seasonal ways are
also recognizable.

And, while own
worn skin is losing
bright colorful gleam,
forest colors are afire.

I wish not to
mesh my eyes with
changing face or
life's color lost.

Please don't let
my frail, faulty
bare limbs lose
vital flowing sap.

I don't starve for
hungry roots of
grasping vitality.

I reason that
seasons are certain as
I see reality in
fall's maturing face.

Chapter III

Measuring Moments

Ancient Parchment

Recently received
love letters
on my writing desk,
speak of
wonderful nights,
days and evenings
spent loving and
being loved.

Morning light
sifts through
open windows as
gentle wind
teases curtains,
creating varying
artful patterns
on desk top.
Dancing light
through thin
woven cloth
causes mind to
wonder.
Sunlight wishes
faithful entrance of
hushed private den.

Morning coffee
gets spilled on
written letters,
brown liquid
soaks like
muddy water,
swamping them
yellow like a

wheat field,
causing ruined
appearance.
Soaked paper
begins to dry,
absorbing liquid
like dry soil
needing provisions.

I think
I see my
lover's image within
shriveled, distorted
paper that
appears like
ancient parchment
on which some
unknown language
written in
blurred penned words
emerges.

Reflective, gazing
minutes bring
further historical
depth of
lamenting time; a
time before
when I had written
such letters a
thousand
years ago
to one who
then as now
captures heart and
mind.

Ancient letters within
memory then
flourish,
allowing vision of
myself and
unvarying
love again.
Ancient words
cause heart to
hear and
liberate
thousand-year-old
written words.

I sit thinking and
reminiscing until
sun reaches zenith,
then until
red evening light
brushes silent eyes.
With stomach empty,
throat dry and
mind exhausted,
I mentally
travel through
ancient times with
long ago lover
who is same as
now.

Hungry Time

On earth time cruises.
Minds celebrate existence.
Day's light engages Earth.
Spiritual realm seeps humanity.

Wheat's golden color arrives.
Time is just in time.
Hunger ignores mouths and stomachs.
Night expects sun's brilliance.

Stalks surrender to thrashing.
Grain is ground and punished.
Bread feeds mind.
Spirits seek thoughtful time.

Tomorrow waits celebration.
Time bakes today.
Bread is never for yesterday.
Hungry stomachs speak now.

Full mouths are silent.
Bread has no enemy.
Bribery is cheap.
Spirits know conspiracies.

Time cruises.
Minds ignorantly celebrate.
Freedom doesn't relinquish cheaply.
Love brings peace.

Crumbling Mind

Near soundless
gnawing of hope,
like termites eating
house and home,
threatens to befall all
I have constructed.

Substance that glues
mind together is
being eaten away,
leaving a weak,
weightless shell of
what I used to be.

Crumbling mind
suspects danger as
I call for help.
I cannot ignore
mud trails and
seasonal flight.

Someone please
call a doctor to
inspect my psyche,
hear gnawing and
save my endangered
mind substance.

Daylight

When my
hands
touch your
face
at night
in dim light,
suggestions
abound;
and when
my heart seeks
more than
an embrace,
do you
read
my mind
and feel
my wish
that daylight
will never
come?

Perennials

My life is
like a garden,
full of annuals.
Few perennials
remain past family,
some disappeared,
some are just
gone.

My beautiful garden
flourishes with
planted annuals.
I remember
not their names,
but recall their
vivid images.
I wish to
see them
more often and
again.

My wonderful
perennial
siblings,
daughters,
son and
grandchildren are
mostly unharmed,
but many of
my friends and
acquaintances are
gone.

I admit to
missing one
precious flower
in particular.
She passed
too soon.
My garden
weeps yet for
her presence.
My garden is
changed.
I am certainly
changed.

Perennial flower
influence is
yet great.
It quietly seeks
my life attention.
It restores my
spirit.
Now a new
mating perennial,
surely blesses
my garden, and
in her beauty,
I see forever
my last seed
planted.

Historical Treasures

I calmly listen while
on a river bank sit,
easily listening to
edge lining trees
wind whisper as a
distant train whistle
grabs my attention.
Diesel engine sound
floats across flat
river valley and
clacking steel
upon steel sound
penetrates humid air.
Remembered
diesels locomotives
on shiny tracks
just beyond a
childhood farm
stirs emotions.
Clacking wheels
greets imagination.
That sound yet
resonates and
draws mental images.
It's a wonderful
emotional semblance,
no matter age or
ability to remember.
Whether it's heard
whistle, tree whisper or
engine roar,
all are soul searching
historical facilitators.

In Time Joined

I seek an
angel kiss,
touch and
embrace.
I bend
time to ever
present be, and
remain as might
on Earth endure.
Hope is built for
present realm,
by casting
bronze statues,
to time wear and
not allow rust.
In sun's stillness,
words are
etched, and
forever describe
two so joined
in steely
minded time.
As civil war
heroes,
we stand as if
yet present,
created from
malleable bronze,
fixed in time.
Shadows and
memories are
now our earthly
salvation.

Listen

I stood at
thick forest edge,
speaking
nature's language
unknown to most.
Birds flew,
vermin crawled,
deer jumped.
They heard
my gentle voice.

I caught a
glimpse in a
scattered eye's
civil presence.
I caught my
breathe on an
icy time edge.
Winter wished to
bury us all in a
cold breathless grave,
and yet somehow
my lung heat
paid a price
for life.

My warm air pushed
through throat,
sound born from
courage alone,
warned all creatures
threatened by cold's
abduction.

There were
no sweet petals,
no laughing plants,
no music within
drab weeds dancing in
bruising wind.
On everything,
winter put a
freezing veneer,
waiting for all to
shiver and crumble.

I am a warning,
speaking of survival,
saying you will live to
see spring in all its
radiant beauty.
I will hold you in
my lap until warm sun
heats us all,
bringing everything
lying dormant to
life once more,
until cool spring
rain bathes Earth
clean of icy
winter memories.

I am your mother,
old speaker of
natural wisdom,
collector of survival
knowledge and
protector of all things
ecologically sound.

Old Clocks

Featureless
yellow faced clocks
cannot smile or
frown.
Their unequal
narrow hands are
not hands at all,
but sharp
little swords
ready to cut and
slash time.
Their hands
cannot reach,
beckon or
draw life closer.
Fearful clocks are
afraid of gawks,
needing only
glances, for
they shun
truth and
need not
reality.
Clocks lie,
cheat and
threaten,
seldom making
anyone happy.
They speak
only with
stoic faces,
risky hands and
annoying little
tick, tick, ticks.

Patience

Oh, where do
roses bloom on time and
patient plants push
calmly through earth?

It's strange how
patience waits and
desires seek a
mountain top quickly.

Dawn takes
its time, and
dusk teases too long,
morning is loving.

Most can't wait for
high tide to meet a
little boat's ambition to
fulfill selfish needs.

Impulsiveness speaks
louder than patience as
anxiety whispers
louder than faith.

Wants and desires
carry no weight, but
dawn and dusk are
heavy influences.

Oh, where do
roses bloom on time and
patient plants push
calmly through earth?

Grinding

All a lonely,
lost soul can do
is stand upon
crushed past and
self-history,
realizing with
open arms and a
listening mind
that only time
will tell.

Only with
pulverizing joy,
can one artfully
gain a feeling of
being a little
self-aware by
grinding foolish
thoughts and
ambitions into
fulfilling sand.

Tricky time sits
on a throne
keeping track of
ever thrashing
life vibrations and
death cycles, for
everyone lives and
dies within honest
wisdom and
true stupidity.

Chapter IV

Feeling
Marvelous

Glass Slippers

I watched
your long
slender shadow
glide across
my floor as
morning sun
sheared through
atrium doors.
On my shiny,
waxed and polished
hardwood floor
you danced in
your glass slippers,
marking and
scraping it,
making patterns
on it as if writing
some ancient
language only
I could interpret.

I read
those symbols and
inscriptions.
It was like
reading tea leaves
in a cup and
finding
my future there,
watching and
loving your
exquisite ballet.

Your shadow
shortened as
morning drifted
into mid-day.
It was as if
our time together
shortened and
glided across
life's stage with
no regrets,
you gracefully in
glass slippers and
I awkwardly in
leather shoes.

We yet found
union in motion as
evening crept
through glass with
its calm darkness.
Our now together
scuffmarks
disappeared from
deficient light along
with our shadows.
They became an
absorbed, hidden
love language in
our polished souls.

Age with Me

Cast no shadows
on fragile love and
doubt not that
flowers yet grow
deep committed,
celebrated roots in
appropriate gardens.

When fading time
holds hand and
accepts a furrowed
face gracefully,
trembling essence
will suitably light a
surviving candle.

Each must lastly
whisper name with
parched mouth,
refrain judgment and
quench thirst with
red wine droplets
seeping from heart.

Each will lastly
soul gaze through
diminished eyes and
lay stationary in
near silent repose,
taking breaths as if
each were last.

Ash and Stone

I silently sit in
melancholy time,
recalling flowers,
how they never
truly leave, but
transform and
finally become
ash and stone.

I wish I had
prayed more in
morning's
filtering light for
I could not have
loved less in
evening's
ruthless darkness.

Flowers on casket
lay dying, while a
sleeping seed waits
another season,
planters and reapers
pray too late for
sun and rain is at
mid-day zenith.

*Melancholy affects tears and smiles, makes a soulful
man scrutinize today while thinking about yesterday.*

Brief Celebration

Soul vestiges
haunt while
moon whitens a
special garden.
Inert swing,
where two lovers
drank coffee,
sits waiting
her return.

Dew soaks
flowers while
moonlight
reflects off
green grass
now blackened.

He mindfully
traces her face,
remembering
every detail.
Down neck
mind flows,
remembering
softness,
fullness,
tantalizing odor.
He recalls
his invited face
between
her breasts.

He dares to
recall more for

her mark
on his mind
threatens to
split his heart.
Remnant thoughts
of her hang
on wet leaves
like reminding
love letters.

Other scents
invade his mind,
defeating
effort to forget.
He dares to
look longer at
lifeless, inviting
garden flowers as
ascending
black shadows
stimulate
leaf edges.

If those
edges were
knives,
he would throw
himself onto them,
be cut into pieces,
then be laid to
rest in same
moon lit garden.

He turns away
from luring past,
turns away
from temptation,

walks under trees,
through
glistening flowers,
past green
empty swing and
under moon light
into empty
blackened house.

He slowly
falls asleep,
remembering
only brief
life and
celebration
traces with her.
She is dead and
gone, and
will never return.

He dares to
rendezvous
with reality and
recall more.
Her mark
on his soul
threatens to
split his heart.
Moon vestiges
remind and
haunt while
black coffee
grows cold.

Drizzling Drops of Love

Meager rain yesterday was
like gentle love falling
sparingly on an inattentive
moisture needing garden.

Favorite flowers didn't grow,
blossoms never appeared,
dry mind couldn't plant or
fix a needed childlike passion.

Gnarly rooted feelings
fostered by gentle hands
couldn't furnish droplets
deep down in earthy crust.

Nature wished to merge
rain and gathered dust of a
lifeless, infrequent love and
renew depth of gathered awe.

Eventually even a drizzle of
love brought growth and
blossom to a heart of dry
darkness and shallow dirt.

Just a little rain brought
radiant growth and bloom
enough to satisfy black soil
waiting to give organic love.

A person needs nourishment enough to sprout roots,
grow and blossom no matter environmental miseries.

Fear Tomorrow

Fear reaches far into tomorrow, past
time's quiet grace, past illusionary design.

I hoist myself
onto tracks
like a train
rushing towards
west coast as if
knowing when
to depart and
what next to do.

I position
loved ones on
my back,
as if stronger
than most,
thinking
I can carry
everyone.

Dreams
sculpted in
washed sand
disappear
without notice
when I reach
ocean's gleam at
waning dusk.

Valor fades and
plans make
no sense as
I ride time
through,
partial sun and
clouds with
melting mind.

I'm thinking
as if tomorrow
might end in a
moment's notice.
I'm living with
washed sand,
false plans and
obligation fear.

I'm a failure,
back at yesterday's
beginning with
loved ones gone,
dreams unfulfilled,
time wasted and
illusions dead in
today's reality.

For Years

For years you satisfied my hunger,
selfish love and adventurous design.

Within your
gentle grasp
lies untold strength,
forever holding
us together.

Each pinch of
salt gives,
life's endless
flavor emerging
with love.

Each physical
touch gives,
love beyond
expression of
shared time.

You know
me well with
salt pinches and
love handfuls
of a great cook.

For years you satisfied my hunger,
selfish love and adventurous design.

How She Made Me

She sits beside me
in sunset light on
our beach watching
last weightless day
meld into heavy night.
I remember when
not together and
I knew loneliness.
She now quietly
lays beside me at night.
Silence owns our
minds and bodies.
Understanding makes
our aging bed.
I remember eating,
sleeping and living alone.

Clocks were enemies and
love had no agenda.
She now holds
morning light in hand,
conquers night with a
reassuring touch.
Oh, how ignorant
I was without her.
Life is now
like a beach,
back and forth,
up and down.
In its water and
sand touching, and
eager splashing,
I find weight,
energy and love.

I Didn't Mean to Make You Cry

I didn't mean to
make you cry when
placing your grandmother's
antique desk and
making space for
you to write and study.

I didn't mean to
make you cry when
preparing dinner with
white candles lit and
wine placed before in
crystal glasses to
celebrate togetherness.

I didn't mean to
make you cry when
passionately writing a
short love poem
about us moving
your possessions into
my humble home.

I didn't mean to
make you cry
when softly saying that
you were wonderful and
that you were, "The One,"
long searched for
until death parts.

Little Things

I touch
her shoulder at
dawn and
see
her blond hair
pillow strewn.
I feel
her rise from
our bed to
make coffee.

My mind
wanders.
I feel
her hand
in mine
when walking.
I sense
her added weight
when swinging.
I feel
her warmth as
she comes near.

Such things are
important and
make me
love her
stronger.
I could mention
other accrued
passions, but

for now,
I shall keep
them within.

On bed side
we sip coffee as
morning
unfolds.
On life edges
we live while
valuing
each other with
new reasons.
I know
her better and
love her more
each unique day.

Lone Rose

Sweet is a lone
red rose bud
found on a
gnarled bush,
severely pruned
too late.

It waited for
summer and
one who would
nourish not harm,
one seeing beauty
not destruction.

I waited for
one who desired
flourishing growth, a
unique rose bush
alone in a courtyard
wishing splendor.

And then came
loving hands,
one who appreciated
flowering freedom,
one who loved
red rose beauty.

Next Visit

I touch an
oak box with
my willful hand.
Your kisses,
hugs and
touches flood
my memories.
My pitiful
caressing hand
burnishes
wood.
Small ash filled
oak box sits
on a dresser.
Morning light
reflects shiny
oak surface.
I fear
my last
contact has
come and gone.
Wing's fluttered
near my ear,
on skin and
in soul.
You were a
rose, a
cloud, a
butterfly.
Mental pictures
yet haunt.
Physical pain
returns as if
yesterday.

I cannot hold or
seek your
earthly love.
You said
good-bye.
I weep and
doubt your return.
Spiritual place is
near yet far.
Quiet is our
once shared world.
Reassurance cannot
invade heart.
I touch
again, and again
that oak box
filled with ashes,
filled with love.
My constant
caressing hand
burnishes
oak wood.
Our together life
went up in flames,
only ashes remain as
next visit hopes
yet plead.

Old Rocking Chair

An old wooden
rocking chair
yet sways, and like time
it remains active,
soothing souls, and
beating back
night fears and
evil demons.
Beyond ample
expression is a powerful
surviving influence.
Only chosen ones
in that place
know its power.
Seems like
only yesterday that
your full lap,
your gentle touch,
your soft words
made an emerging
world sensible.
You have passed,
leaving rocking
to another,
like ashes to ashes,
power to power,
rocking to rocking.
That old wooden
rocking chair doesn't
same sway, and
can't equally soothe
my soul like when
you rocked
me as a child.

Passion

Passion is buried
like eager spring
corn souls or
inflexible fall
walnut spirits.
Buried passion is
lost until provoked.

Waning thoughts,
fake smiles and
pretend gestures
leave bitter taste, and
say nothing useful,
make day impotent and
night unborn.

Many are like a
sleeping seed
seeking liberation.
Most times remaining
beneath a warm
protective mental
crust like a seed.

Days motivate
forever and
nights linger
temporarily.
Blackness often
speaks louder
than light.

River Has No Banks

A river has
no permanent
banks or
limitations
when relentless
rain has its way.

Natural ways
make earth seek new
resistance paths as
might rivers
seek solace for
being innocent.

To love gently
is speaking calm
river ways and
to love strongly
is bonding with
persistent passion.

And when eroding
love shapes and
evolution remakes,
humanity ever
flows like a river with
no permanent banks.

Rose Thorn

A simple man
knows a rose's spirit,
thorns have pricked
his vulnerable mind,
heart and hands that
dared to approach
perceptible beauty.

A rose bush
deepens life and
lifts caring to a
weighty influence.
Innocent bushes
accept praise, but
not thorny guilt.

True love surely
conjures harm
like a rose bush's
spiritual thorn
draws passion,
knows beauty and
shows love.

A loving touch
can draw pious
blood from an
anxious hand
that picks and
presents with a
silent rose wound.

Softness

Let your
thick hands
softly lay beads
around my
delicate neck.
I need your
clear cool
water beads
flowing through
my life.

I'm soft inside.
Night sorrow
needs mending,
so, speak gently
to me now.
Your gifts are
enough for anyone
waiting, but only
colorful enough
for gentle me.

You are my
apt spiritual
water beads and
I'm your willing
soulful amulet.
Lightly place
yourself in
my loving care,
passing time,
tolerant life.

Suntan Ribbons

Thank you glowing
sunlight that decorates
our morning bed, and
captures our hearts,
minds and souls.

Sought mid-day sun
that tans our skin and
heats our hatless heads is
waiting just outside.

Wished for elusive
lazy afternoon glow
begs a long nap,
weights our eyes and
teases our drowsy minds.

Sweet dusky sunset
makes its presence
known soon for
sun only romances and
touches during day.

Our tanned bodies
soothe romance and
host our loving minds
on a deviously lit bed
thoughtfully waiting.

Darkness caresses
our warm souls and
soothes our intensity for
radiant time has brought
us delicately closer.

Tender Thoughts

Tender thoughts
on mind's edge,
float like
small sail boats
seeking port.
They threaten
to arrange
my disposition
soft and
pliable.

I realize that
simplicity can
smooth and
polish rough
reflective stones
with wind
driven time and
with gentle
collected
water drops.

Strange are
days when a
river calls
my name and
speaks to me in
naturalness as if
I am a
tree or a flower
seeking refuge in
tender thoughtfulness.

I listen and
grasp for
near time with
empty hands.
I rearrange
immediate
thoughts and
place them into
slots with tender and
attentive mind.

I hear river
giving substance and
direction.
My flat-bottom boat
disposition finds
no threat of
mean river arrogance.
It benevolently speaks
tender thoughts and
I lovingly listen.

*To navigate mind's edge without fear and see
reflected face on river's surface is enlightening.*

Vibrations

My vibrating being gong resonates tranquilly
Like a bell tolling escaped sound forgivingly,
Like a chime being cast from molten iron gladly.

My soul seeks like a cool meandering stream,
Flowing while thinking, brooding and recalling,
While quenching belief expansion and reduction.

My mind nurtures earth empathy and wisdom.
It is like a glorious cosmic vibration converting
Black inner chaos into white external harmony.

My heart surely senses love shuddering changes
While discovering another equal vibrating gong.
Together we toll an original heartfelt resonance.

*Cosmic vibrations are around and within all tenuous
human beings whether they seek own humanity or not.*

Chapter V

Accepting Motion

As If Knowing

Spring sometimes struggles,
Leaf resurrection unveils,
Nature invites servants,
Birds fly in time and space,
Trees knowingly contribute,
Earth schedules spiritual time,
Great are horned owls,
Birds perform aerial dances.

Mozart's music is internal.

Wind beats trees into submission,
Wind is passionately flowing,
Compliments create growth,
Owls stare out of wonder,
Witnesses hide in thickets,
Stoic gazes present boldness,
Trees give an intelligent persona,
Two examples are enough.

Romantic lullabies are for hearts.

Earth surely calls seasons home,
Intelligence sits in open spaces,
Deer live as if knowing enough,
Spring is always on time,
Mothers have a majestic realm,
Everything has soul,
Most flowers seek sunlight,
Human beings are not in charge.

Earth is a harmonious stepping stone.

Rose Bud and Thorn

Dusk's shadows
disappear like
life memories as
mementos resign
to existing time.
Brief slinking
daydreams
flow past
present time
into midnight.

Dawn naively brings
false hopes and
artificial faith
to accumulated
recollections.
Illusory shadows
pretend daily life
exists repeatedly
while teasing
unconscious time.

A final sunset
breathes its
hot last breath and
willingly washes
hands and feet of
those who hold and
walk with vision.
Good-byes always
get absorbed by
earth and sea.

Collected shadows
gained and
mementos saved
satisfy most
realistic minds,
but imaginative
humans seek
sun and moon,
gather dreams,
pursue visions.

Some live as if
tomorrow
forever exists and
resides between
rosebud and thorn
without fear.
Life to them is
never as easy as
breathing air and
watching shadows.

Seldom does time
live in misery
waiting around a
next day corner
full of anger;
often it sits beside
us in harmony and
full of advice
concerning itself
and tomorrow.

Black Back Curve

My white sandy beach
stretches miles into
tomorrow it seems,
like a white ribbon
tying coastal pine trees
together or like a
dividing line separating
earth, sky and sea.
       Small waves gather to
       share brisk wind.
       Many shore trees are
       hurricane torn to
       once appearance.
       Dolphins play
       closely off shore.
       I see their backs
       out of water and
       occasionally a
       displayed tail.
       I wish to play,
       enjoy their games,
       but no invite comes;
       besides, cold water
       would make
       me shutter in
       northern Florida.
I once lost time while
walking ribbons and
noticing dividing lines.
I sadly must return
to Indiana tomorrow
where patient winter
is yet teaching lesson
about cold weather.

Calendared Cycle

Did you hear those
wary leaves fall?
They came sailing
on dry rushing wind
like miniature ships
tacking on open sea.
Red, brown and
gold lifeless leaves
ignorantly sought a
resting place to be.
They were silently
discarded by
sturdy branches where
millions gathered for
summer transfiguring.

They bravely abided
one legendary season,
flourishing, dancing
and living free in
hot summer breezes.
But, then cruel fall
slowly approached
all living things.
Leaves too soon
became falling
organic material.
Mother's natural
ravenous mouth,
let nothing escape
her calendared cycle.

Change

Change arrives
Somewhere between
Peeking horizon light and
Breaking dawn sun,
Scattering pleasant
Radiance to
Day seeds in
Fertile night gardens.
Nature's artillery light
Kills defenseless
Distant black horizon,
Flashing and
Bombarding
Gardens to life.
Battles brew on
Wayward plains as
Distant horizon light
Forever seeks to
Illumine while
Darkness tests
Willingness to abide.
Light is void without
Defining darkness.

o

I visited my muddy
whispering river
again yesterday.
Her yielding
banks were
somewhat different,
water was a
little higher,

faster and
muddier.
It never remains static
for new and
different water
always passes through
its embracing banks.
It whispered to
me as usual, but
in a different tone.
It was like a mother
giving advice or a
friend gently coaxing
me towards a decision.
I noticed a gentle
southern breeze
bucking little waves
of resisting current.

We seemed similar,
river and me,
flowing with
least resistance,
gradually changing
with whispering advice.
It, however, seemed
content to serve own purpose
in forever time as if
eternity willed it so.
I then truthfully was
less content for
my purpose seemed
more dubious,
flowing towards
tomorrow against
resistance, but with
some self-control.

Dramatic Dance

In early warm
afternoon sunlight
on an open green lawn
near a dense wood, a
wild male turkey
danced a mating ballet.

He gained mild attention
of a female turkey while
ignoring fascination
from a human voyeur
hiding behind a near
building with a camera.

He puffed feathers,
gracefully posturing
with tail plume spread,
giving a magnificent
display of nimble
natural male beauty.

His long white
feathered neck
stretched as
striking red comb
hung brilliantly in
dazzling sun.

Gray feathers moved
out while dragging
one huge wing.
Graceful motion
blended with desire
to be appreciated.

Rejection was
unacceptable for
his dance and
flaunted beauty
was irresistible
even for a camera.

Finally, into forest
they sauntered.
His wonderful dance
seemed complete.
Her relenting heart
was certainly won.

A seasonal ritual of
natural romance and
his dramatic male
turkey mating ballet
had surely captured
her imagination.

Enlightenment

Please open minds
to a world waiting
restoration, to a place
where abuse awareness
lies woefully silent;
where hurtful words are
placed in drawers and
lies are left hanging.

Many adults favor
angry weeds instead
of beautiful flowers, and
are like a hailstorm
beating, crushing and
ruining fragile flora,
leaving destruction
in offended minds.

o

"Acceptance," rides a
white horse,
needing feed and
water, with spurs
digging deep into
vulnerable flanks.
She grills meat
until overcooked,
making it burnt and
extremely tough.

She's stern as a
saddle placed with a
girth too tight.

She rubs sores into
accepted abused places.
Change is coming and
enlightenment is not
pretty, but abuse
acceptance is
awareness repelled.
Bruised faces,
broken bones,
shattered hearts are
recognized and
mended.

o

So, speak no more
accepting words,
sing no more
approving songs and
live no more
tolerating days.
In a better world,
"Enlightenment,"
gallantly rides
abusing plains,
restoring love.

Child abuse
acceptance is
hopefully waning,
finding a place
where spirits,
minds and
hearts know
worth, and that
all children are
precious flowers.

Mindless Wind

Somewhere wind
finds a home and
lies naturally dead.
It finds a place
to never travel or
be beneficial.
It just passes and
whispers no more
in a waiting world
that wishes peace.
Wind seeks to
adapt, obey and
reform with
flaws and strengths.
It behaves while
seeking mercy as if
blindly following
some secret plan.
It makes love
some days and
destroys much in
its path other days.
Love and fear,
benevolence and
wickedness define
its personality.
And yet,
powerful sun
creates wind,
enslaves it and
makes it a
mindless captive
servant of a
higher power.

140

Nature Whispering

A new morning
bursts with
spring green.
Pleasant flower
odors fill
crisp clean air.
Newness wakes
my senses as
faint dawn light
unveils day.

Fully expectant
flowers and trees
yet silently drip
morning moisture
from night rain.
Birds in trees and
quiet air sing, and
communicate
with me as
I try to translate.

Thus, I ineptly
speak of natural
beauty when saying
good morning.
I reflect while
standing in midst
of nature's awe,
writing unworthy
poetic lyrics
to bird melodies.

Orange Moon

Through lush leafed
tree branches a
full orange moon
illumines my world.
Mind wanders and
imagines a giant
orange daylily
blossom hanging
in a black sky on
year's shortest night.

I cannot sleep
for my driven spirit
is like those distant
howling coyotes,
seemingly laughing
at an orange moon.
They are covertly
calling from some
distant phantom
hunting habitat.

I also appear
to be invited to
another place
on an imaginary
foreign planet.
I ignorantly feel a
spiritual linking
with motivating
vastness flaunting
itself amid illusion.

I surely belong to
that moon,
those stars, and
that constantly
beaconing universe.
Arms spread as if
embracing that
universe through a
night moon and
mindful illusion.

We are similar,
wild coyotes and
introverted me,
for in our feeble minds
we constantly
hunger for something.
They seek infinite
food for stomach.
I seek finite spiritual
sustenance for soul.

I can nearly hear
angels singing as
coyotes serenade a
bright orange moon.
I feel spirits and
angels near
beneath that
orange moon.
Peace lingers
within my heart,
mind and soul.

Outside

Rain outside
reminds and
conjures images of
forgotten days.

It's like noticing
time and
each droplet is a
precious second.

They gather as
paragraphs and
then as pages of
vivid memories.

So many words,
paragraphs and
pages flow, and
gently calm me.

Night offering
outside window
peacefully puts
me to sleep.

By midnight, a
novel is written, a
song is sung, a
day is fulfilled.

Peeking Sun

Twilight peeks
through golden
tree leaves as an
awkward season
searches for a
place to belong.

Summer is
gone, with
its heat and
leisure attitude,
almost forgetting
way back home.

Winter seeks a
known presence,
gracefully sculpting
ice and snow
with a hostile, but
artful attitude.

All is due to that
graceful light that
morning peaks and
evening speaks as
Earth's adoring
caretaker sun.

Man is a leaf and
Earth is a season.
Small things
change quickly and
big things
change slowly.

Part 2

The Art of Self Liberation

Introduction

Life matters little if lived without self-expression and liberty. Life is cheap if constructed from imitation thoughts, knowledge and philosophy. A thoughtful deed given with realized awareness is less valuable than one accomplished with ignorance of success; and yet privately, self-awareness is required for true public giving. Humility is balancing actions on a sharp awareness fulcrum. In final analysis, one's true evaluation is the responsibility of others.

Academia is a wonderful foundation, but has no walls or roof. Self-construction is possible only when accompanied with experience and wisdom. Everyone must construct own house and write own story in own way and about own experience.

Life, liberty and the pursuit of happiness is a near spiritual thing on Earth, but surely based on heavenly advice. A collection of personal life poems, written or unwritten, give legitimacy and proof of one's life.

Some types of ignorance can be beneficial if practiced with the right state of mind. Sometimes lack of knowledge is a good thing. Child-like innocence breeds wonder and the gift of true awareness. Questioning seeks answers. Doubt leads to discovered faith.

Life is successful when learning and following most rules, but with an interrogating and rebellious mind.

Chapter VI

Saving Memories

Melancholy Music

Melancholy music,
even as a small child,
allowed memorable days
of joy and discovery,
passion and energy
blended with harmony.

I didn't let anyone steal
my moods or joys or
destroy daydreams;
I was in a place where
reality was temporary and
prospects were infinite.

I lived on a midwestern
family farm pursuing
happiness for many years;
it was where corn grew,
ponies dotted pasture and
mother hugged me often.

It was a dynamic place
where brother and I
listened for locomotives,
sister gave advice and
father communicated
manhood principles.

Melancholy influenced a
prevailing disposition
that instilled confidence
in myself and a future of love,
freedom and faith that only a
resilient family could edify.

Night Fell Reluctantly

Night fell reluctantly
within my essence.
It felt soft as if
wishing to be
my friend, and
like a friend,
it loved and asked
for full attention.
I became sleepy,
put head down
on a grassy knoll,
beneath stars and
rising moon.
Night sky sprinkled
conspiracy and
made me feel
spiritually clean.
I rubbed my body,
wishing to bathe
in its benevolence.
I caught cold
midnight gleam as
ghostly frost
condensed and
seeped into mind,
body and soul.
I became one with
night and slept on
cold accepting ground.
It pulled heat from me.
I never woke, but
became one with
cold earth and
pleasant hyperthermia.

Colorful Wings

You are light and shiny polished brass.
I am oak wood with blue lining velvet.

Our relationship is
eagle wings and
white cirrus clouds.
We come together
knowing each other
in a melodic place.
Wonder greets as
faith soothes while
peace prevails.
We are trumpet and
wooden case,
offering music.
We are like two
colorful wings
of a golden eagle
flying effortlessly,
feeling each note
as if a feather,
distinguishing
each feather
controlling
our poised flight.

You are light and shiny polished brass.
I am oak wood with blue lining velvet.

Spilled Salt

Be like
spilled salt
on a white
table top,
nearly
disappearing
in a colorless
domain.

Be voiceless
salt of earth,
silently
blending while
adding flavor.

Let others
speak of
difference or
use here and
there.
Let others
speak of
your quality,
zest and
worthiness.

Artifacts

I artfully burn
family memories,
throw them into
trash cans and
give them away.
I do, however,
keep some and
carefully put them
in small boxes and
deep containers
to most likely
discard later.

It's funny how
objects spark
memories and
guilt, and how
discarding them
hampers moving on
with my life.

I manipulate
sorrow as a
mildew laden
childhood
aerial farm picture
disappears in
flames, and
rusty nuts and
bolts accumulated
by my father are
given away or
put in an old
tool box for myself.

I cannot keep
that for which
I have no purpose.
I balance time,
space and regret
while I sort,
trash and
justify burning
my parents last
useless artifacts.

I sadly ask for
forgiveness as
memories haunt.
Grief yet seeps,
while smoke
rises and
trash cans fill.
I fear that
I'm making
my deceased
parents cry.
I shed tears
recalling faces,
staring at flames,
watching memories
disappear in
rising smoke.

It's like last
remnants of
my mother and
father's lives
being cremated
on their home
rock driveway.

Observation

To not convey
observed
life mysteries
allows anxious
descriptions to
fall between
mind fractures.

True observation
defines most
everything as if
being positive or
negative, like
magnets seeking
balance.

Observation
opens a grand
wisdom gate and
puts shame to
ignorance of
not learning
until old age.

It's like a
cat warning
with signs of
danger to an
ignorant mouse
not knowing
shock of instant
death threat.
Observation
makes minds

advance and
hearts leap for
reasoning of
even little things
that confound.

Angels observe
planets aligning,
stars dying and
old men dancing
their last days in a
winter snowstorm
before heart quits.

God observes
positive and
negative with
gravitational awe,
stars being born and
old planets' last
celestial effect.

Answers lie in
irreplaceable
observation that
defines whole
of a graceful life
ending with
collected wisdom.

My World

Moonlight
painted mind
while I slept
last night.
Thunder later
crashed above
my little
gray house,
rain filled
birdbath and
watered
garden.

I silently
slept while
my world
changed with
shifting noises to
suit itself.

I morning
awakened and
stepped outside
into nature's
graceful
expression of
flowing creation.
Sun and breeze
refreshed
my mind and
revitalized
my spirit.

A Few Degrees

Five-day-old
snow yet
lies motionless,
not drifting or
melting, only
shrinking slightly,
getting ignored as
eyes get familiar with
it causing no harm.
White turns to
gray, then black.
It will soon be gone,
transformed
without effort.
Temperature
wavers like an
enemy teasing
death with only
its presence.
Little changes
can be monumental.
Unseen power
can strike an
element dead.
A few degrees
up or down,
left or right,
in or out;
can make a mind
wonder and a
life disappear.

A Tear

I studied
rainbow colors
gleaned from tears
while I thought
about sorrow.

Sunlight glistened
on a wet cheek, and
I calculated
tear meaning and
repercussions.

I measured life
through tear width,
depth and length as
it came to mind and
I got educated.

I absorbed
knowledge and
gained wisdom, but
seldom analyzed
my own tears.

I finally moved
beyond observing and
measuring, and
learned to feel and
display tear causes.

Clear Creek Stone

Oh, how many times must
I tolerantly ask for help?

I'm a creek stone
waiting spring's rush
to transport me
further downstream.
Spring is near, only
melting snow and
hammering rain
can help me move.
I can't dislodge self
from a fixed place.

Oh, how many times must
I tolerantly ask for help?

It's freezing here,
waiting with no choices.
In my patient world,
nature works slowly
it always seems, but
then that is only
my humble opinion.
I'm only a stone
waiting for needed
promise of physics.

Oh, how many times must
I tolerantly ask for help?

I'm an ignorant
entity with little faith.

Yet deep within
my cold hardness,
expectation exists.
It's strange how
I can nearly see
downstream,
feel soft water's
sympathetic caress.

I can almost
imagine tomorrow,
being carried by
unknown forces,
polished by creek's
altering experience.
Maybe I'm not
just a stone, but a
Godly piece of a
living creek.

*Oh, how many times must
I tolerantly ask for help?*

Complicated Times

Complicated times
bring baffling storms,
seeking answers within
howling mind wind.

Drenched hopes and
disturbed dreams come
in a heartless tempest
of thrashing wind.

Most people are like a
solitary meadow tree
courageously standing
against pending wind.

o

My understanding
of existence eludes
eyes wishing to see and
heart wishing to feel.

My wayward essence
seeks wholeness and
one to say sorry as if
apologies bring order.

I seek an amiable future
like a lone meadow tree
resigns to and accepts
pending wind forces.

Eat at My Table

Scorched lives sought inspiration for freedom's rebellion,
    like a need for selfless kindling encourages a fire.

Mental scraps and bits of soul knew essential demands,
    like air discerned evolving heat from raging flames.

Inspiration was like meat placed on a smoldering fire and
    roasted for a banquet of hot thinking wayfarers.

Thanks to those who came near and far to indulge liberty
    on a Sunday morning of philosophical sunlight.

Brilliant writings gave nourishment to life as breaking of
    bread and drinking of wine incited relationships.

Hundreds gathered at an elongated oak table as peaceful
    spirituality awoke in prepared minds on Monday.

New beginning and thoughtful ending solutions distinctly
    furrowed numerous statesmen's thoughtful brow.

Food for thought became meat for a mental liberty fire
    that grilled justice for all on an activist Tuesday.

And, to think it all began with an invitation to dinner,
    some thoughtful kindling and a freedom match.

Glass Bowls

Tinder questions
gathered in a
silent bedroom as
darkness emerged.
Sleep begged
engagement, but
thoughts were
more like a murky
sermon of words
spoken on a
Sunday morning that
warned against
sinful participation.
Words were like scarlet
vocabulary fruit
rotting in a
glass bowl.
Fretting sermon
fought to find
spirits teaching
about figs and a
mountain fruit tree.

o

I sang and
picked praise
like a drunken sailor
finding land after
drifting at sea for
seemingly years.
Soon morning
sun in eyes and a
rushing breeze

through window
caught my attention.
New light and
new hope
caused me to
think of
new plans.
New life
answers emerged.
I danced to
music in a
renewed head.

Old glass bowl
broke into a
thousand pieces.
A tree of
life grew as
I stood on a
mountain top,
seeing, breathing,
eating.
Fruit never
tasted so good as
I fell asleep and
slept like a baby
near my lover.

Miller's Stone

Beneath soil's
crust, I felt life's
swelling delight of
growing roots,
then golden stalk,
then precious grain.

Within an inventor's
mind a machine
was designed and
welded together to
thrash and separate
me from my chaff.

I surrendered to a
natural miller's
crushing stone that
transformed my
ordinary essence
into purified flour.

Children's hunger
gave worth to me as
I became bread in a
place where no one
knew my name or
sought my origin.

Along with others,
I became hope, and
in this feeding of
ten thousand children,
I matured with them,
I became holy.

On Strident Glee

Doors open to
What might be
While courage
Pleads expression of
Life, liberty and
Pursuit of happiness.

Today's sunlight
Renews and
Casts shadows over
Yesterday's dreams
For those seeking
True enlightenment.

Life gives a
Feeling of
Exhilaration
Through swinging
Doors with
Light streaming,

Time refuses
Incarceration for
Enlightenment glows,
Vision seeks and
Liberty flows
In its beauty.

Awkward Earth dances to sun's weightless harmony.

Chapter VII

Hearing Music

A Classic Book

I found my spirit
lingering among words,
lost in paragraphs written
for small children.
I found myself on
soft linen pages with
black ink that faded,
smeared over years from
ravaging humidity,
wet fingers turning and
clumsy hands holding.

I was never famous,
on a best-selling list or
known for my creator.
I was unfortunately
like an undeserving
grape that was never
fermented into wine,
or a lonely cumulus
cloud that ineptly
never produced rain.

I at last became a
significant antique
silently enduring life
among known classics.
I was situated on a
high shelf to be more
than persistent words.
I gladly became an
unassuming, well-read,
remembered narrative.

A Few Glorious Years

My springtime
is surely ending
like concrete
blocks made of
broken sea shells
or like brittle pond
ice melting,

My old graceful
athletic body
once upon a time
progressed over
high hurdles
like ocean waves
finding their shore.

I journeyed on a
galloping steed
across Earth's
dangerous realm,
weighed life's
worthiness with a
weathered soul.

Gold and silver
purchased freedom
from a waiting,
mean gallows, yet
I strolled amid a
shaded park as an
alien desperado.

When leaves in
fall became ash,
no one knew
my name because
my tenuous life
failed any kind of
graceful expression.

Noisy ducks on
that melting ice
lectured me well
for being such a
proficient fool
while leisurely
forging self-glory.

And now my cheap
headstone will be
made of sea shells,
slightly leaning with
no inscription that
well explains all
with no excuses.

A Plead for Sun and Rain

Mind meadows
ripple with
grassy ideas,
unwilling to feel
cutting blade of
mowing society.
They stretch for
miles and miles
into yesterday,
boldly learning and
tomorrow fearfully
anticipating.

I prayerfully
plead for
rain and
sun on a
grateful dare to
seek a place where
no one has
gone, a
place where
new grass
grows in
filtered sun.

I crave for
basking within
Earth's offerings as
they stretch
towards a
new horizon.
My spirit
surpasses spring,

summer and
fall as
revelation comes
into view.

I journey
into winter,
starting all
over again,
pleading for
sun and rain,
pleading for
spring,
pleading for
growth,
pleading for a
cutting blade.

Mind meadows
ripple with
grassy ideas,
willing to feel
cutting blade of
mowing society.
They stretch for
miles and miles
into tomorrow,
boldly learning and
yesterday bravely
forgetting.

Aging Years

When I reached
fifty aging years,
reality struck
like a soft mallet,
gently at first, but
slowly increased to a
rhythmic pounding.

It finally matched
my heart rhythm.
I learned to
count beats as if
having a certain
number, and was
on second side of total.

Soon I counted
many things,
such as
turn signals,
church bells and
ticking clocks.

How well,
now I know,
God is a
mathematician,
counting,
counting, but
in His case,
counting such as
rain drops, hairs,
galaxies and
universes.

Then when at
sixty aging years,
reality struck again,
gently at first, but
then tougher as wisdom
increased in rhythm.
I forgot how to
count such things as
birthdays,
decades and
seasons.

Reality finally
faded into
remembrance and
I began living
in some fantasy
place,
where there were
no clocks or
ways to escape.

I exclusively
count blessings
these days at
seventy aging years.
I wonder what
I will be counting at
eighty.

As If I Have a Brain

It's strange how I can now speak as if
I have a brain, as if I have a soul.

Time's soft
cool rain
continues to
rust my face,
my body,
my very being
when history
didn't destroy.

Out of once
beautiful steel,
carefully processed by
unbearable heat and
constant pressure,
I was formed into
an artful statue.
Master foundrymen
cast and created an
iron base fit for a
king upon which
I silently stood.
I was placed in a
respectful courtyard
after being shaped,
formed and fashioned.
Appreciation and love
surrounded me.

I thought I would
respectfully
last forever in a

courtyard of heroes.
I was then
woefully ignored,
left behind
like an absurd
forgotten dream.
My iron feet
gradually dissolved.
I soon became
rusty, toppled and
half buried in soil.

I silently spoke
mind as if
having a brain,
heart and philosophy.
I shed inner tears that
caused further rusting.
I pretended that
nothing made me
unhappy, after all
I was a pretend
man of steel.

Time seemed to be
my only enemy.
Flakes of red rust
like bloody
soul pieces
abandoned me.
I feared to be
soon no more.

It's strange how I can now speak as if
I have a brain, as if I have a soul.

Be a True American

Be a true American.
Be a true
representative.
Be a true
soldier against
progressive thieves of
freedom and
states' rights.
Please vote against
careless spending,
lost liberty and
deficit suicide.
Please take more
leadership and
be a true
representative of
people not party.
Fight against
Socialism.
Take away the
arrogance and
prideful cohorts.
Please fight against
egotism and
government control.
Please fight
against tyrants
who believe
they are doing
good for society.
Be a true American.
There's a revolution
brewing.

Beasts of Conscience

Beasts of conscience
smashed through
many heart fortresses
some time ago;
like charging zephyrs
on a wild rampage,
they soiled minds and
pelted fragile souls
with revived malice.

Perverted heads
composed and
reiterated songs
that led astray
innocent minds and
sought evilness
like a huge sponge
soaking blood on a
slaughterhouse floor.

Odd mental visions
frightened and
cruelly veiled
foolish humanity;
red lights blazed and
green lights churned
mixed signals behind a
impervious curtain
begging empathy.

Young people
danced no more to
forgotten songs and
hidden freedom;
glory got replaced
by shouting
mean words that
pierced ears and
garnered mortality.

Surely angels knew
what to do with all
those defeated lives;
perhaps transform or
reform them into
spiritual beings,
kindly allow them
to hover awhile and
then to heaven drift.

Bravery Trudged

Bravery came with
lantern lighted way,
flaunted golden ray
upon a beaten path
on which I walked
with a heaven sent
rescue trained man.

My shaky hand
reached for own
antique lantern,
rounded handle
worn smooth.
Its metal felt like a
soft weighted kiss.

I followed his
shadowy profile
stepping before me,
gladly following
his silent leading
footsteps and guiding
silhouetted corona.

He steadily trudged
onward showing no
fear while instilling
found bravery within
my spinning mind;
time and path split
for both to go own way.

o

I shook his hand with
recently acquired
intrepid awareness,
for in that spiritual
daunting night need,
I found new born
courage within myself.

    Seeing a guiding
    lantern within self
    can light ways to
    progress alone on
    frightening paths
    with no retreating
    from a shadowy future.

Changing Joy

Mist in distant
muted trees
shapes and nurtures
my disposition as
sweat soaks
nominal clothing.
Homemade
ice cream is
eaten fast, yet
drips from spoons
outside in
needed shade.
Tree foliage creates
a canopy for
grateful heads.
Two short-lived
hot weather
week episodes,
twice a summer,
must be endured
with grace and
few complaints.
Too soon
cold fronts and
silent flurries
will change
my attitude, and
give nature's
temperament a
frosty pardon.
Summer's heat and
cool reprieve is a
wonderful Midwestern
changing joy.

Clearly

Not so clearly do
we see sunsets,
color of skin or
hear spoken hellos.
Not so clearly do
we perceive other
unique worlds, yet
speak minds with
awkward grace and
listen impatiently.

Clearly, we
need more help than
character provides in
negotiating rooms, on
smoky battlefields or
at war cemetery plots.
Clearly or imprecisely
we often distinguish
best and worst of
precious mankind.

*We ignorantly anger fast, hear wrongly, point fingers
quickly, yet clearly and gradually we repair humanity.*

Curly Tail Blues

Fear and desire make
terrible friends on a path
leading towards disaster.

Someone put another log
on an already hot fire,
for a celebrity was coming
to an outdoor banquet.
Invited guests expected an
ugly face on a pig roaster.

Joey Bear loaded a gun,
made one shot count.
Curly took a red-eye
train to heaven with
original B-B-Q sauce
spread over his fat body.

That old man surely knew
how to roast a pig after
calling many to dinner and
singing Curly Tail Blues.
It was strange how many
became curly tail feasters.

Fear and desire make
terrible friends on a path
leading towards disaster.

Deep

Imagination seeks many
middays full of sunshine
and soaked midnights
full of accompanying stars.

Like an injured shoeless foot
or a tanned shirtless back, a
mind without daydreams
is ominously found naked.

Unlike an adrift thought or
or a sadly amputated foot, a
strong back can sustain a
lightweight load effortlessly.

Mental burdens, however,
can instigate injury like a
dam nearly bursting or an
oak tree bending too far.

Without shoe and shirt or
thought and support, a
graceful human being also
requires mental dexterity.

Daydreams often clothe
fantasy thoughts, but a
brilliant mind fabricates
imaginative achievements.

Define a Life

A glimpse of
human spirit
caused empathy,
like a thousand
lit candles on a
bright afternoon
created hope.

A decision to
strike a match to
benign candles,
defined heart and
changed life as
God merged and
enlightened me.

Easy movement
of an antique desk,
love seat and a
glass topped table,
outlined days as did
two feather pillows
redefine nights.

Our minds touched
in darkness while
learning to live
together as might
two eagles ascend
warm current and
equally land safely.

We found
mutual respect,

contriving a nest
in a dense forest of
defined humanity,
like a thousand trees
defines a forest.

Security was found
in a warm place
where we huddled
on cold nights and
spoke of greater
two together than
lesser two apart.

Two safer worlds
silently merged with
gathered light as
one decision caused
new incentives to
light more candles
for years together.

Humanity is a lit
candle struggling
to stay alive.
We found that two
candles together can
ignite a thousand
adoring candles.

Drawn

I was drawn
into
life's flow,
like feet
to river's
edge,
pulled and
pushed
by something
wishing to
change
me into
muddy debris.

I acquiesced.

Life became
easy,
flowing with
least resistance as
agile feet
stopped kicking,
strong arms
stopped stroking,
finally doing
no more
than drifting with
free mind and
faithful soul.

I acquiesced.

Drifting

I gently place
my head on a
white pillow and
then mind drift
without notice
like yesterday's
snow clouds.
It's strange how
silently watching
slow moving time
can be fruitless and
can make nagging
goals disappear.

I yet pillow drift,
continuing through
ignored sound and
waning metabolism.
Heart beat slows,
breathing shallows;
awareness seeks a
melding of all in a
gray stifled place.
Worries melt like
dreary snow as
warm mid-day waits
for no one.

I easily become
no one in particular,
nothing in reality,

for unquestionably
I have discovered
formed essence and
beguiled humanity.
To seek solace
from pillow drift
makes tough days
seem feasible and
long nights
tolerable.

I am surely
pillow liberated and
thought unleashed,
freely drifting on
water filled clouds,
seeking a colorless
snow white place
to mentally repose.
I am readily purified
like an eternal spirit
associating with
terrestrial creatures
in heaven.

Dusty Mind

I try to shake dust from
My soiled mind.
I count grinding days and
Nights on a road to
Chicago.
My truck died and
My feet went flat.
My home
Disappeared and
My father said,
"Behave."
I yet hear his voice while
I stand here alone.
I feel his hand touch
My shoulder as
I listen to advice.
Farm is gone and
Farming doesn't exist
In my modern life.
Present dust is
City grime,
Diesel soot and
Red brick erosion dust.
My mind seeks
Some dusting off
In a new time place.
I yet recall
Lessons learned as a
Child and
Young man
Groping for a
Good cleaning of
Collecting soul.

Gallows Wait

No one perceives
strong-willed blackness
creeping towards a
blue sky possessing
few lingering clouds.
Rot and decay deface
gray wooden gallows
waiting another neck.

Someone will die
from a splendidly
tied shiny hemp rope
expecting business.
Calculated weight,
distance and stature
statics silently wait a
professional's opinion.

Guilty verdict spreads
like wildfire through
hearts needing revenge.
But, Justice hides
her empty eyes and
dry wrinkly hands that
will prayerfully tie a
hangman's noose.

Revenge emerges
beneath that blue sky
as transparent thought

wanes with sunlight
seeping felt sorrow.
A convicted man
silently weeps while
forgiveness fades.

Nearby temple grace
imparts understanding,
crime clutters minds and
vengeance threatens a
response if justice doesn't
soon find a home in front
of a courthouse that
silently endures justice.

Spoiling gallows
sorrowfully speaks with
historical murmurers.
Ominous black clad
authority slowly
absorbs a carefully
planned and swiftly
executed demise.

Gloves

I grab some gloves.
It's cold outside.
Snow will not melt.
I walk slowly.
Mind juices are sluggish.

There is no hat.
Age seeks snow.
My hands tremble.
My soul quivers.
I yet here Dylan sing.

My truck roars.
Pipes are loud.
I take curves too fast.
My future is windowless.
Cold air freezes mind.

What a way to go.
My life is frozen.
My spirit is rigid.
Off go my gloves.
Wings spread.

I hear heavenly spirits.
I feel warm all over.
I am forgiven.
I am quiet.
No need for gloves.

Good-by Momma

On a cold hard table
he willingly placed
throbbing head.
Hunger gnawed at
empty stomach of failure.
No diet of confidence or
self-esteem applied.
Courage was destroyed as
poisoned mind and body
sought destruction.

Classroom lights
glared through
watery blue eyes.
He pulled gray
comforting hoody
sweatshirt overhead.
Authority spoke,
forcing a self-imposed
dark mindful
restraining place.

As one left behind,
fallen and discarded,
he didn't belong.
He was a throw away
worthless article at
sixteen and lived
in an unhappy world
that knew trash.
He lived up to
low expectations.

So, he said good-bye to
yellow brick
road of dreams,
grew up hard and
fast with a
violent streak.
He said good-bye to
smoky-booze breath
Momma in cheap
perfumed clothes.

He stumbled
out of school door,
out of mean home,
walked from a
world of demise.
He was lost
between cracks,
forgotten by school,
loving Mamma and
mean society.

How does an aimless kid abruptly say good-bye to his
smoky-booze breath mother in cheap perfumed clothes?

Chapter VIII

Finding
Maturity

Silently Waiting

Giant maple trees
stand silently,
waiting wind's
loving caress.
I too wait for
loving wind to kiss
my anxious lips.

Art laden foliage
puts hand upon
my shoulder,
speaks of history,
passion and
expectations with
rustling leaves.

I can nearly hear
my life purpose and
manipulation of
blessed gifts for
trees can teach and
I can learn from
nature's intentions.

Innate trees have
plans for shape of
intricate branches.
They have leaves
numbered enough to
seize each season as
natural art pieces.

I also have innate
plans for shape,

branches and leaves.
I also have ability
to please and
lend wonderful
cooling shade.

Both trees and
I know how to let
life be free and feel
wind in appendages,
naturally waiting
with joyful shade
in artful grace.

My own artfully
laden foliage
puts hand upon
other shoulders,
speaks of history,
passion and
expectations with
rustling mind.

Sneakers and Boots

Tightly laced farm
shoes were exchanged
for cherished black
Converse sneakers
that allowed me to
effortlessly run like
notorious wind across
green pastures and
down narrow paths
with eight-year old legs.

I noticed cloudless,
unpolluted sky as
sun casually baked
my skin brown.
Knee-high July corn
stretched to sky like
me growing taller as
warm, humid breezes
caressed face and
mussed hair at age ten.

I rode a Shetland pony
fast and hard with
worn cowboy boots
on growing feet while
herding imaginary cattle.
I talked cowboy to
pretend cowboys, and
ate baked beans from a
small metal plate with a
large wooden spoon.

I nearly always
learned and applied
reliability on that
Indiana family farm
during those amazing
days with sister and
brother loving me
for what I was, and
gentle parents teaching
me about what to be.

I was a developing
dichotomy of sorts,
switching sneakers
for cowboy boots,
being patient with
conjured dream.
I was impulsive about
awakening manhood,
casting adult shadows with
an eleven-year old body.

I later traded boots for
basketball shoes,
gave up my pony for a
fifty-four Ford sedan.
Onward and upward
my contrasting heart,
mind and soul
mystically developed
by willingly exchanging
one thing for another

Aren't We All Visitors

My friend Steve
was a
bad ass army
Green Beret for
six years in
Viet Nam.
At forty-two,
green attitude
yet flowed in
his veins.

I saw cookies
on a near table
begging to
be eaten.
He offered one.
It was good,
homemade by
his mother,
baked especially
for him.

I called him a
mamma's boy.
"Yes, I am,"
he said,
"Aren't we all?"
I replied,
"Aren't we all?"

Most men
deep within
maintain a

piece of a
little boy psyche
and when gone,
one becomes
all man, but
surely something
then is missing.

As tough as
Steve was, that
little boy part
surely remained.
A dichotomy
probably lived
within him, but
then life itself
is a web of
dichotomies.

*I called him a
mamma's boy.
"Yes, I am,"
he said,
"Aren't we all?"
I replied,
"Aren't we all?"*

Still Stones

"Respect our strength because it overwhelms vulnerability with solid foundations that supports humanity."

Towers stand tall,
steel bridges span,
highways traverse,
therefore modest
still stones celebrate
great usefulness.

Definition of each
type of still stone
has classification
through civilization's
pragmatic use and
idealistic beauty.

Earth patiently waits
opportunity to share
its seemingly endless
artful importance and
concentration with
impatient mankind.

"Fear not fellow stones for we are a courageous, evolutionary element of a billion foundations, pylons and roads of civilization."

That's a Joke

I took another
playbook page,
put it into action and
was taken for a loss.
I foolishly thought
life was a game.

There were many
serious people at
my front door,
hinges were worn,
knocker didn't
work anymore.

Knuckles got broken
as curiosity pounded
day and night as if
they had something
vital to say about an
obsolete playbook.

I quit playing games,
pretending to have a
helmet, some pads,
an NFL attitude and
fight to gain yardage
on a visitor's field.

I said, "Don't come
to my front door
looking for a player.
My hinges are worn
and knocker doesn't
work anymore."

Uncle Charlie's Diary

I pressed
my smooth
respectful hand
over frayed
cloth corners,
rounded by
too much
handling and
rubbing of
Uncle Charlie's
diary that was
bound paper
with a soft blue
cardboard cover.

It was full of
pictures, stories
and poems about
his Indiana
childhood and
those who
brought him
to manhood.
Grand warm
loving days
bound within a
book of dry
yellowed pages,
sought air and
my attention.

Wide eyed
gawking and
attentive reading

revealed that
Uncle Charlie was
not so different
than naive me.
"Thank you
Uncle Charlie,"
I whispered,
"for delivering
history to me."
I put his tattered
old prose in a
secure place.

o

On a safe shelf
now resides
Uncle Charlie's
bound life and
time story,
free from more
handling and
rubbing, yet
living innocently
on discovered
historical yellow
book pages of
forgotten prose
to never again
be neglected.

Sharing is Personal

You ask for
truth and
support, and
with little
insight I give
wanted advice.
You wish not
negatives so
I spin positives.

I open mind to
sensitive side
while absorbing
haunting reality.
I interfere when
you have needs,
for you ask and
listen better than
noisy me.

You understand
reasoning and
are like me, but
I need to get in
step, for sharing
is most personal,
especially between
two who know
each other well.

Entertaining

Life's influences
came and went,
like pounding
beach waves,
brilliant thoughts,
flying feathers and
good-bye kisses.

I secretly
wrote songs,
picked strings and
sang about stories.
It was therapy
many lonely nights
while at home.

I finally got a
cheap gig at a
local bar,
played one set
three times and
learned an artist's
tough plight.

I painfully
sang songs for
three nights
until it became
excruciating,
then retired from
entertaining.

Entertaining is easy if you have talent.
Socializing is easy if you're an extrovert.

Insecurity

Insecurity drives
false boldness,
speaks loudly and
boasts of unknown
knowledge while
confidence sits
quietly waiting on a
spinning world to
enlighten, and
make light as if
day approaches for
no reason.

Anxiety speaks
half-truths and
distorts facts like
corrupting weeds
while confidence
seeks answers and
tends garden soil as if
flowers ever belong.

Insecurity is timid,
yet somehow
survives and
catches sight of
another day's
delight or
says to hell with
it all, and
remains in still
bemuse while
night creeps and
day seeps.

White Silk Laid Hush

Fair garments
lay on still
yielding body.
Timid flowers
surround unashamed.
Rose petals
in a sundial's shadow
help measure day.
      Thoughtful family
      measures grief.
      Tranquil hands
      lay white silk while
      silence sleeps.
      Beautiful clothing
      decorates unwilling
      short lived beauty.
            Swollen deep
            sorrow is managed
            like a contained river.
            Fractured minds
            tremble with pain.
            Garments fade,
            flowers wilt as a
            child reaches for
            heaven's gate.
                  She looks back at
                  ashes created by
                  own white adorned
                  sleeping hush.
                  She gracefully touches
                  other minds and
                  smiles inside her soul.
                  She butterfly-ascends.

Words Enough

My acute ears
heard a world
louder than
could be
imagined.
Majestic
mountains
spoke to soul
from fifty
miles away.
They called,
tempted and
filled me with
wonder.

My poetic
writing journey
began with
one deep gaze,
one felt thought,
one written line.
Through
grand eyes,
I cherished
scenes and
gained notions
that put me
in untrained,
poetic awe.

I became a
bearer of truth,
recounting a
million revelations.

I prayed to be a
profound poet
with memories and
desires, and
ability to share
my surging
essence with
other people as
if being a
speaking river.

I yet pray
for an admirable
conclusion to
my treasured
alert moments and
prolonged days.
Surely my poetry
gives expression
well enough to
at least calm one
troubled soul,
let one mind see a
river's serenity or
at least satisfy me.

True expression
yet evades
my passionate
distillation.
Mindful insight
remains spitefully
confined.
My torture is
eyes that see,
ears that hear,
heart that feels, but

my mind only
partially coalesces
inner essence.

I sit restricted
by own flaws,
frustrated by
own ignorance,
hampered by own
poetic injustice.
I'm like a man
with no legs who
wishes to walk
or a man with
blind eyes who
wishes to see.
I need poetic
cerebral solace.

I fear that
I shall be heading
to heaven before
my work is done,
before my poetry
books are read,
my carefully taken
photos are noticed,
my life stories are
remembered for a
few generations and
my philosophy has
meaning to someone
other than myself.

Working Hands

Damaged hands
tenderly touch a
lover's supple face
with near reverence.

Fallen rose petals uniquely affect beyond lingering thorns.

They are working,
callused hands
that carried loads
long and afar.

They are abrasive
like sandpaper and
yet thoughtfully
warm and tender.

They are creative
hands that shaped
worldly things with
artful deliberation.

A lover's face is held
in those hands with
abiding gentleness
felt within a heart.

Fallen rose petals uniquely affect beyond lingering thorns.

God's nature of affairs
contrast everything like
roughness and softness,
men and women.

Worn Face

Deep creases
on a
worn face
waited
for a brawl
to begin,
like a black
storm on a
distant horizon.

Foes haunted
like a mean,
conjuring
storm
approaching
with inevitable
thunder
and instigating
lightening.

Heavy
face creases
deepened
with thoughtful
concern that
seemed as
inevitable as
looming
storm.

Misjudgment
of rival gang
information,
humanitarian

knowledge
and street insight
transcended
common sense and
destructive power.

Fighters
stood
in near
blackened streets,
threatening
with guns
extending
affecting
meaty hands.

One man
asked, "Why?"
as a huge
toothy smile
graced
his face,
then expanded
into warm
friendship.

A part-time
peace keeper,
mediator
and common sense
man,
diverted war
with only a
worn furrowed
face.

Four Stones

Three silhouetted
grave stones on a
hill horizon rest
half buried from
harsh freezing and
thawing time.
Many gather to say
hello and good-bye,
for a cemetery is a
place to remember
flesh amid stones.

Weather worn
names and
dates silently
convey little,
like muted past
time markers.
History begs
tribute on a
bitter cold day
where few are
left to visit.

My Earthly mark is merely a stone's
silhouette on a grassy knoll at sunset.

A spirit grips
my hand and
escorts me
like a caring
mother.
Another spirit
brushes

my thin gray hair
and initiates
feelings of
liberated time.

I hover over a
newly placed stone
while reading
own epitaph.
It sits straight and
level on newly
evacuated soil
just a few feet
from those other
worn stones with
same last name.

I ghostly rest for a
transitory while as
dusk engulfs Earth,
absorbs silhouettes,
hides four stones
communing in a
voiceless graveyard.
My weightless
spirit willingly flies
with a persuasive
heavenly embrace.

My Earthly mark is merely a stone's
silhouette on a grassy knoll at sunset.

Stones

Throw down
stones carried
too long
while waiting
justice.
Let your
eyes feast
on her
assuring
pose,
holding a
level scale.
She came
forth with
brilliant
gesture and
grace in
morning
light.
Prayers were
answered,
justice was
served,
minds were
changed.
Punishment
fit crime.
Go home,
hand
in hand,
brush a
mother's
tears.

Chapter IX

Using
Mentality

Chapter IX

Using
Mortality

Bold Letters

Recovering
bold words
written in sand
to someone
who sought love
long ago is
like a hand
steering clouds.

o

To trust revenge and hatred
is a worthless endeavor
with no relief, for one cannot
remove a heart's damaged day.
To let greed and selfishness
speak lies at a church revival
is giving evil space in a
Sunday morning mind.

Unfortunately, time strolls
down a wayward road with
scuff marks on its essence.
Passive words seep into
dead roots waiting to be
removed and hauled away.
So, let time's dirty hands be
brothers with their grimy feet.

o

A beach where
I first wrote
letters of
joy and love
disregarded
history's
accounting of
temporary me.
I steered no
storm clouds
with a pretentious
hand,
sought no
revenge
because of
neglect, but
was ashamed of
my dusty feet
that wished
divine washing.

I am so Crude

I cut and
gathered
wheat stalks
in arms,
to later get
grain from
beating,
flour from
grinding and
bread from
baking.

I wished more
life from
eating,
energy from
digesting and
fertilizer from
defecating.

I wished to
enrich earth
with my life
processes and
plant again
seeds for
my sequel.
I'm crude and
too organic,
but how else
might I live?

Braided Thoughts

I intended
silence while
humbly sitting
with intricate
mind toiling,
weaving raw
thoughts,
musing woven
solutions.
It was like
braiding hemp
into a naive
hangman's noose.

My complicated
mind created
time and space
strands that
coalesced into
tainted reality.
Even expertly
braided ropes
wear and fray,
become weak
and useless, but
my silent mouth,
noisy mind and
weighty body are
ever crafting a
hangman's noose.

Evil thoughts and
harmful words
make my innocent

roped mind weep.
Wetness falls on
my tying hands,
seeking to simplify
reasoning.
I fall to knees
in a prayer,
wishing to not
climb a mental
gallows with
misplaced actions.
I wish not to
need redemption
or saving of soul,
but I know
it's coming.
I wish not to
think about a
hangman's noose.

I fear I am my
own hangman,
braiding own rope,
tying own noose.
Innocent thoughts
mingle with
stranded solutions.
My intended
silence and
braiding mind
yet ever tie an
accountable
hangman's noose.

Cool Rain

Cool rain in
delicate mind
soaks an expanding
world viewpoint.
It grows flowers anew
as my calm mother
speaks to me at age five
in an upstairs room
at bed time telling
fascinating stories
never heard.

o

Playful images in
in melancholy mind
re-live a
childhood existence as
steady cool rain falls
outside my window.
It seems to revive
childish imagination,
mislaid memories and
blooming ideas that
yet cultivate in my
maturing psyche,
delicately planted
by my sweet mother.

Gratitude

I'll always sense
with grace of time,
my daughter's realm
within own realm,
soaking wind, rain
and gratitude.

I amazingly sensed
my daughter's
familiar essence as
night and day passed,
and she grew and
made me smile.

Life caused her to
struggle against
winds blowing in
upturned face and
rain falling on
embracing arms.

I used to sense
her needs when near,
but time and distance
separated our
loving connection,
but not our love.

I'll always sensed
with grace of time,
my daughter's realm
within own realm,
soaking wind, rain
and gratitude.

Heavy Booted Mind

A big man
walked a
planked floor with
heavy boots
trailing mud.
His blazing fists
across a face
too many times
forged hatred.
His mighty hands
shaped a mind
as sure as a
farrier's hammer
upon a steel
horseshoe formed.

Nothing artful
came from a
malleable
young mind after
applied heat and
quenching cold
shaped it.

A judge asked,
why such a
mean streak
prevailed and
why such
destruction
surfaced.
He questioned
why such a
boys' mind

could not
control itself.
That new big
booted man,
red hot
steel forger
of shapes,
answered not.

Down inside
he was a
father replica.
A son who
could also not
scrape mud from
his heavy
booted mind or
reshape his
soft malleable
disposition with a
hammer.

In Another's Eyes

You painted my mind blue for too many years
        like a single-minded artist with only one brush.

You created a portrait no one appreciated, and artfully
        burned our house down with spilled solvent.

I too red flame burned into gray ash, yet my fragile spirit
        remained to display self in another art form.

In a graveyard of brilliant colors, eyes watered, and with
        sorrow, hearts reasoned a better place for me.

Now in grace of an infinite canvas, I'm painted anew,
        for I became a masterpiece with blue angel eyes.

Knowledge Light

I eagerly sought
a full moon's
visible transparency
through bedroom
window entering,
but could not grasp
shadowy awareness with
restrained mind.

It was like a spirit
searching my room,
traversing night,
wishing for an
entrance to
impart badly needed
knowledge to an
incompetent mind.

Knowing not
true consciousness,
I half-awake slept,
surely unaware of
moon's inclination,
seemingly searching
my malleable
unassuming mind.

I discarded
moonlight fantasy,
remaining in
night's darkness,
learning that known
ignorance is easily
accepted with an

uneducated mind.

I finally opened
my wary mind,
full of wonder and
intrigue, but
could not grasp
superior mystical
wisdom without an
instinctive mind.

Into early morning
I half-asleep strove,
full of desire, but
unwilling to work.
Moonlight passed,
leaving me without
divulged wisdom in a
confining mind.

"What a waste of time,"
I daytime whispered,
thinking it was a
dream that taught
nothing, except
possibly wonder and
intrigue of a superior,
mystical mind.

Life Knowledge

Born are lights
that shine within
gray matter
beneath a red
river's meander.
It's a place
no one knows
except God
who shares it
only with angels.

It grows like a
fresh journey
finding itself,
seeping like a
creek from a
distant spring.
Mystical mind
travels through
brain mazes with
least resistance.

Mind voyages to
unknown parts with
no known return,
incredibly glowing
like an eager firefly
lighting a small
dark world part
while expecting
hundreds of willing
cohorts to help.

With humble
beginning, from
natural firefly to
innate human;
nothing, no one
has knowledge of
what there is to
learn, illumine or
how far a river
flows to its end.

Monumental
life knowledge is
magically gathered
like lush grapes
to someday be
transformed into
wine, drunk with
friends and
pissed away in a
festive caldron.

Mind is that light
of humanity
that shines within
majestic body,
spirit and soul
with a red river of
meandering blood.
It's a divine place
that only God
knows how works.

Sharks Deep

I caught my
breath on a
high cliff edge,
saw too far into
intricate mind.
I dove into
deep ocean,
searching for
infinite answers
while water
dancing with
hungry sharks.

I feared
becoming a
sailor's bones
stripped of meat,
laying deep in a
complex subject
never solved.

I also feared
being one who
forever weeps
regretful tears,
offering only
salt to earth's
percentage.

My mind desired
to high-cliff-dive
and be careless.
I ignorantly said
be not afraid of

sharks for they
have no brain,
have no teeth and
can't smell blood.

With deep breath
on a mental
cliff edge,
I recklessly
dove far into
intricate mind,
deep into a
vast ocean with
brain seeking
infinite wisdom.

I was a fool
who had no fear,
listened to only
self and shaped
my voyages with
misaligned stars.
I was alone on a
seemingly calm
mental ocean
waiting for a
white squall to
take me down.

Again

Down an aware
reality path
I crawl,
covering eyes,
holding breath,
unable to
clearly speak,
wishing to
possibly ignore
menacing truth.

I pray not
to hear
inner voice
speak altering
hard reasoning
words that
might ask
me to keep
moving and
not look back.

I dare to part
fingers placed
across eyes and
take a deep breath
to wholly consider
what I fear, and
thus, choose an
alternative path
towards which
to bravely veer.

I don't want to
change, yet must
pragmatically
stand strong and
proceed quickly,
seeking that which
bends mind,
swells heart and
naively causes
my spirit to soar.

Slumber Party of One

I seek no
glorious journey,
but solutions to
where I might
silently travel and
tease mind
to dream.

Maps seem to
seep and soak
while I sleep.
In wonder in
amazement,
mind believes
all is possible.

In morning when
I awaken,
answers and
solutions appear.
In night's black
air comes
silent wisdom.

I think it comes
from a connection
to heaven or
another planet
where answers
grow like edified
flowers.

Wisdom grows
in a garden that

angels and
spirits tend.
So, glory be to
amazing ways of
mentoring nights.

I wish to thank
mystical sleep or
whomever speaks
my name and
tells angels that
I am worthy of
answers.

I shall willingly
share what is
given from deep
space or deep
within myself
during slumber
parties of one.

Sources don't
matter as nights
consume and
days resume as if
zero was shared and
little ensued while
traveling to genius.

From where does knowledge gained by accident come?

Composing a Song

I drift in river's
liberating flow as
impatience often
disturbs serenity
like rock music
aggravates geese.

I wish an oar with
which to paddle
to accelerate trip,
yet I know a long
journey lies
beyond fatigue.

I gaze skyward
allowing sun to
warm face, then
pass under a rare
tree shadow that
provides shade.

I listen and
try to predict life
obstacles ahead as
wise river whispers
melodic sounds and
I compose lyrics.

River seeks own
speed, distance and
rhythm as we share
combined destiny and
exotic ending to a
continuum river song.

Chapter X

Cherishing Moods

Air We Breathe

*Life ultimately and
literally takes
our breath away.*

Air we breathe is
often ignored and
oddly most times
unimportant, yet
it gives precious
body fuel and a
chance to harvest
fruitful efforts,
like jumping
high fences or
running through
flower gardens.

Air nourishes
our beasty lungs,
makes them feed
magnificent body,
wanting more and
more as we gamble
with calculated time.

*Life ultimately and
literally takes
our breath away.*

Consumed air
takes us home,
let's us exercise
Earth's bounty,

let's travel
towards every
frosty morning,
warm dusk and
clear night under
stars and moon.

We habitually
breathe deeply and
expectantly exhale
until air importance
is finally realized,
vitally praised and
spiritually thanked
when near last
evaluating days.

*Life ultimately and
literally takes
our breath away.*

Lost Courage

They felt fear
become part of
themselves, yet
courage meant
everything.

It carried them
against cold winds
like geese winging
southward in
November.

Wise men spoke
of nature and
watched triangular
sky trails fade
in distant light.

Some men were
like geese winging
in inert fall air,
helpless to lead
or fly point.

Courage gained
useful confidence.
War should have
started long ago,
was said in review.

Too many
turned eyes and
allowed evil to
eat goose meat
too long.

And then in July,
courage found
confidence and a
brave battle
ensued.

Yesterday always
contributes to
today's proof of
tactics to utilize
tomorrow.

Trident men
that soared high
in a battle of
sunlight gleam
were gallantly led.

Arrogance

Liability sleeps
naively beside an
innocent man,
instills dreams and
fixes haunting
artificial ideas.

>Arrogance is a
>gradual thing that
>creeps upon a man
>like a quiet rain
>beginning with
>self-centeredness.

>Celebrity doesn't
>advance wisdom or
>impart knowledge,
>just as speeches and
>close groups don't
>prove competence.

>Ignorant yes-men,
>yes-press and
>yes-votes don't
>mean yes when
>tent poles and
>canvas get moved.

>Humility stands
>in warm rain with
>waterproof boots,
>new umbrella and
>all-weather gear
>all made to order.

Arrogance
ultimately lies alone
in a cold night bed
while schemers wrap
rain repelling gear
around themselves.

Liability sleeps
naively beside an
innocent man,
instills dreams and
fixes haunting
artificial ideas.

*Crowd adulation is a curious thing that diminishes at
an outside political rally in an unpredicted cold drizzle.*

Chisel or Flute

I seldom chisel at
my unfair attitudes
that often appear
through ignorance.

Ignorance mars.

Prejudice knocks at
my closed door and
speaks softly before
my mind screams.

Change upsets.

My culture feeds
defying positions
that create activists
seeking fairness.

Forgetting taunts.

My drum beats to
marching flute music
that inspires ignition
of freedom torches.

Equality pleases.

My instrument,
whether chisel or
flute exposes and
influences others.

Forgiveness speaks.

Colorful, Yet Dying

I hear sad leaves crying,
falling upon themselves,
while thirsty ground yearns
for those natural friends
who went notably down
while others are declining.

War is surely evolving as
known life is hesitating,
fearless young people with
collapsing minds know time
is running out to escape
being unsung heroes.

Old men in a worn group
extend fat fists towards a
utterly clear blue sky as
politicians argue about
whether some young men
should certainly go to war.

Even though a beautiful
flag of stars and stripes
in all kinds of weather
waves its adorning self,
sad bald eagles weep for
values are disappearing.

Nearly everything seems
undoubtedly reasonable,
but attitudes are fading and
clear ideas are losing luster,
democracy is withering and
time is clearly running out.

Crowded Universe

Sun traverses sky with specified perfection of
Earth's 4.54 billion years old initiated math.

Solitude is creative and
doesn't accelerate or
give false conceptions.
Sun's solitude frightens
static minds as much as
hard fixed river boulders
threaten smooth canoeing.

To shoot white water rapids
on a bright sunny afternoon
requires skill and confidence.
To see stars visible during
day is insightful mental flow.
To navigate a precise mind
makes ancient numbers glow.

Cosmic principles perfectly
flow out there in a black
boulder-strewn universe.
Man must calculate with
telescopes far and near to
navigate an alien cosmos
in a speed-of-light canoe.

Sun traverses sky with specified perfection of
Earth's 4.54 billion years old initiated math.

Flowers than Weeds

I placed
here and there
those things that
made me cry,
planted them
with caring
thought as if in a
garden so large
I couldn't see
another side.

And, now as
I stroll garden,
I seldom see
any resulting
sorrow growing,
only floral
mutations that
appear more
like flowers
than weeds.

Some memories are best forgotten weeds, replaced by
deeply planted annual flowers in a vibrant garden.

Freedom's Song

A liberating
melody and some
intertwining lyrics
coalesced with
rhythmic ocean.

I tasted salt and
experienced a caress
while standing on a
long white shore
I called majestic.

I finally wrote a
unique love song
that surely altered
my essence as I
sang it to another.

I surpassed hope
while lovingly
holding her hand,
singing our unique
love song.

Oh, how fragile
we were while
talking, smiling,
laughing and
ignoring time.

Earth's rhythmic pounding drove sense into my life,
like hammer seeking nail, like wave shaping sand.

I kept writing
on that shore, as
if she were sun,
waves and sky
horizon colliding.

I wrote many
more inspiring
shared songs,
embraced love and
tasted her salt.

My liberated
mind merged with
her rhythmic clock
that matched our
pulsating spirits.

I heard and felt her
long after sunset,
in places where
melody and lyrics
lovingly intertwined.

My love songs
melded into poetry,
my beach got
revisited repeatedly,
time kept recurring.

My inspiration
for a taste of salty
Earth's rhythm
never surpassed
my love for her.

I Called Her Sweetheart

I put down
damaged books,
dulled pencils and
musical toys
aptly made for
children, and
picked up a
black sleek
work of art, a
nine-millimeter
machine
made for war
with eight
pretty, shiny,
lead-tipped
brass kisses.

Grand were
adoring thoughts
felt with power
in hand.
I loved her
black dry mouth,
cool smooth
skin and
odor of
protective oil.
She caused
feel good sweat
on hands and
brow as
I caressed her
privately.

I couldn't
forget her and
called her
"Sweetheart,"
made her center
of my unstable
attention.
I held her
lovingly and
watched her
like a black
storm cloud
wishing to fuel
her German
fashioned,
subdued world.

I whispered
her name during
chilly, lonely
nights and
tried to quell
my full of rage
obsessed mind.
I gently laid
my throbbing
head on a
night pillow
and placed
my sweetheart
beneath that
feather pillow
to help me
sleep at night.

Melancholy

Melancholy is
self-reflection,
like weeping
is necessary
on a lonely,
abusing night.

Artistic
melancholy is
liberating,
not depressing,
serving as useful
soul fuel.

Introspection
causes rise of
living history
wishing to
resonate a
gloomy song.

Historical
melancholy
vividly recalls
experiences to
put present life
in perspective.

It's like singing
or playing a
blues song,
feeling comfort
by finding a
reason to cry.

271

Metaphor

I see marks on an
oak hardwood floor,
showing stimulating
life images while
I write poetry at an
antique walnut desk.

I see satisfied faces,
climbed peaks and
experienced storms
that provoke curious
golden floor images
nailed into place.

God seems to wink,
smile and muse mind
as if teasing me to
perceive hidden,
faithful thoughts
on wooden planks.

I finally confess to
introspection demand,
letting myself laugh at
seeing God's created
metaphors artistically
appear in etched grain.

My New Name

*"You're a leader of cohort angels
fighting against earthly evil spirits"*

I close
wet eyes, and
see regal faces in a
cloudless sky.
I slowly tilt
head and
hear shrill bells,
ringing from a
far temple,
freely echoing
my new name.

I drink
whisky bottle dry,
forget speaking
mind of
relished thoughts
gained willingly.
I whisper,
"Forgive my
beastly ways for
I only seek a
way home."

I fix mind as
outlook changes.
My callused
knees ache,
brawny back burns,
captured heart
throbs.

Rushing doves
crash in air as
edgy evening
sings good-bye.

I hear
advising lyrics,
"Make a pure
home in a
fearless life
with holy
wisdom."
I know not
what it means.
"Your name is
Arishmina."

"You're a leader of cohort angels
fighting against earthly evil spirits"

I am now
more than a
new name,
new mind and
new life way.
I am a renewed,
revived phantom.
I hear bells
speak and
see doves
on ground toil.

Nine Gap Questions

Is it possible that
universal controllers
operate between
humans and God,
playing spiritual wars
from some high perch?

Are our lives much
like a small mouse
darting in some woods,
methodically moving
from one hiding place
to another hiding place?

Are all journeys long and
especially dangerous
for a defenseless mouse
if a curious, hungry cat
is hunting and feels
like altering a life?

Is a curious cat happy if
it moves towards a
mouse for a closer look,
catches, then plays,
kills and finally eats that
warm mouse for lunch?

If a mouse could think,
wouldn't it understand
forces beyond present and
know something greater
than a place to hide and
simply exist in its world?

Can a lowly mouse
abandon ignorance and
embrace something greater
than "mousedom" and
grasp that another world
exists beyond trepidation?

Does God sit on a
high backyard swing,
watching humans and
mean cats play with and
slaughter witless mice in
His holy calculated way?

Is there a small gap
amid humans and mice,
amid life existence and
death arrangements,
amid mice creation and
mouser destruction?

Are there mysterious
powerful, middle cats,
universe operating at
many sanctified levels,
constantly watching and
consuming for God?

Pure and Honest

Within genuine possibilities of
a rarefied glowing life,

magnificent sunrises and
sunsets are infinitely noticed

in profound mind fissures
of idea, thought and dialog.

Glorious nature ever whispers
colorful historic accounts of

rational beings mutely heading
towards intrepid nights that

begin and end with blackness and
cannot be overlooked.

Insight fosters white wisdom,
untruths favor black ignorance

and both glorious day and
night seek enduring attention of

rare glowing minds saving
secrets and mending reasons.

Nothing is like day and night,
everything seeks gray thought

that can foster pure wisdom
and review honest ignorance.

Epilogue

I Became

I became an
archaic man
before my eyes,
learned that mirrors
didn't lie to eyes;
they first showed a
pure baby then a
brash young man.

I too soon
became an aware
Earth citizen;
a mellowing
educator of
young children
while life
inevitably cycled.

I saw images
display time and
normal thoughts
organize life as
spirit collected a
million events that
showed aging of
surviving-self.

Still pictures
confirmed aging
face through
unwilling eyes as
personal history
was wondrously
contained in an
ever active soul.

I was my own
best witness to
creation and
eventual demise;
my rise and
unwilling fall
humbled as
I witnessed all.

Wrinkles and
sagging skin,
fragile bones,
ground joints,
faulty heart and
stressed lungs were
all unbelievably
presented.

Mean time's
reflection of
life experiences
finally made
sense to me
while witnessing
own personal
demise.

About the Author

I am the result of a life time influence and compilation of insight, foolishness and spirituality with a bit of wisdom occasionally surfacing. I grew up on an Indiana farm and never forgot my roots, even though I was involved with serving the Navy, teaching, manufacturing, real estate and construction during my seventy-six years of life. My wide variety of experiences are philosophically and spiritually woven throughout my writing of poetry.

I have experienced joy and sorrow, enlightenment and ignorance, pride and humility; thus, my writing expresses protected passions and emotions connected with life's diverse passing of time and collection of encounters, events and coincidences. I have a melancholy sense of personal and family history. Sometimes both hurt and reward me to a point of causing inner and outer emotional expression.

The cosmos seems to speak to me as if I have been to Earth before or possibly from somewhere out there in that mysterious cosmos. I speculate that heaven is only a thought or a moment away. I believe that I am only a grain of sand in the desert of humanity. I consider myself unimportant in that desert, but know without me the desert would be less. So, in my final analysis, I pray to be important enough to get God's attention.

Printed in the United States
By Bookmasters